PRAISE FOR
THE FORGOTTEN EXODUS
AND BRUCE FENTON

"*The Forgotten Exodus* is a timely, thought-provoking, and extremely useful little book by Bruce Fenton. Fenton's arguments, and the impressive body of evidence he has assembled, fly in the face of the very powerful—and for the most part uncontested and unexamined—scientific consensus that *Homo sapiens* evolved exclusively within the African continent and spread outwards from there within the last 70,000 years or so. Unquestioning acceptance of this 'out-of-Africa' reference frame is to be found everywhere in the relevant scientific literature."

> —GRAHAM HANCOCK, internationally bestselling
> author of *Magicians of the Gods, Fingerprints of the
> Gods,* and *America Before*

"This 'exodus' back into Africa coincided with many cultural developments such as the first signs of art and advanced hunting technologies like the bow and arrow. Could it be that people from Asia came back to Africa and brought their genes and ideas with them?"

> —*FORBES*

"Fenton's case beckons every reader intrigued by the origins of humanity to take a closer look at the preconceptions underlying the firmly established out of Africa theory for *Homo sapiens.* Well worth reading and thinking about for a long time to come. Highly recommended—five stars for such a clear-cut case for a fundamental theory that may reshape the scientific understanding of human evolution."

> —MICHAEL CARMICHAEL, historian of science and
> former senior US presidential campaign advisor

"Bringing together vast areas of research and the latest discoveries, the author questions everything we have been taught about human evolution and the subsequent populating of the world by modern humans. Turning the accepted paradigm on its head, Fenton provides us with a new model of human evolution and migration that demands attention."

—*NEW DAWN MAGAZINE*

Foreword by Erich von Däniken
author of *Chariots of the Gods*

EXOGENESIS
HYBRID HUMANS

A Scientific History of
EXTRATERRESTRIAL
GENETIC MANIPULATION

BRUCE R. FENTON AND DANIELLA FENTON

NEW
PAGE

This edition first published in 2020 by New Page Books, an imprint of
Red Wheel/Weiser, LLC

With offices at:
65 Parker Street, Suite 7
Newburyport, MA 01950
www.redwheelweiser.com

ISBN: 978-1-63265-174-7

Library of Congress Cataloging-in-Publication Data available upon
request

Cover design by Kathryn Sky-Peck
Interior by Happenstance Type-O-Rama
Typeset in Warnock Pro, Oswald, Bourton, and Trade Gothic

Printed in the United States of America
IBI

10 9 8 7 6 5 4 3 2 1

*To the children of Earth,
especially Camilla,
Ariane, and Zackary*

If you're not ready to find exceptional things, you won't discover them. Of course, every argument needs to be based on evidence, but if the evidence points to an anomaly, we need to talk about an anomaly.

—PROFESSOR AVI LOEB, chairman of
Harvard University's astronomy department

CONTENTS

CONTENTS

FOREWORD

Charles Darwin is regarded as the father of evolution. In certain circles, questioning his theory of evolution comes close to committing professional suicide, despite the fact that for years highly respected scientists have warned against the belief in the theory of evolution. So did Bruno Vollmert (1920–2002), a professor of molecular chemistry at the University of Karlsruhe in Germany. He wrote, "Darwin's theory of the origin of species and of life in general by mutation and selection was and is a great mistake."[1] Nobel laureate Francis Crick shared similar opinions, as did astrophysicist Sir Fred Hoyle and math genius Chandra Wickramasinghe (the latter being director of the Buckingham Center of Astrobiology, Buckingham University, England).[2]

Forty years ago, I had already added an idea to the discussion that is becoming more and more realistic today: the intended, artificial mutation from outside. Originally, the idea did not come from me at all—I had taken it from the Holy Scripture, the Bible. There, in the first book of Moses, chapter 6, verses 1–4, is talk of "sons of God" who "took daughters of men as their wives." Thousands of years later, Christians believe in the "virgin birth." The mother of Jesus is said to have become pregnant through immaculate conception by the "Holy Spirit." But who thought up the original idea of this artificial insemination? In the Old Testament, miracles are reported in several passages. The infertile women Sarah (Genesis 18:10–14) and Rebecca (Genesis 25:21–26) were fortunate enough to have been visited by some heavenly beings. But this "seed from heaven" was a matter of course in the ancient Orient. Each ruler had to be of "divine descent." Otherwise, he was worth nothing. The Egyptian god Amun-Ra impregnated the mothers of his heirs. Alexander the Great (356–323 BC) was said to have been conceived by a thunderbolt. The Assyrian king Assurbanipal (687–627 BC) was a son of the goddess Ishtar. Akkadian king Hammurabi (1728–1686 BC) is also considered as one of the heavenly births. His mother was impregnated by the sun god. Figures such as Buddha or Zarathustra have been conceived by a "divine ray" in the womb of their virgin mothers, just as was the founder of the Tibetan Empire, Gesar, or the first of the mythical emperors of China. The same applies to the original rulers of the Inca or the Aztecs.

The motif is an ancient one. In the Babylonian Gilgamesh epic, which dates back to the Sumerian civilization, Gilgamesh, the king of the city of Uruk, is created by the gods. "Thus Gilgamesh was created by the great Gods: eleven cubits was his height . . . two parts of him god-like, a third of him human."[3]

It may be argued that all these traditions of heavenly births have sprung from the imagination of our ancestors. They just wished for something like that. But with that, we are only making things too easy for ourselves. The oldest writings are from Sumer: the cuneiform. The earliest scribes, who made thicker and thinner marks on their clay tablets with some type of stylus, were not science fiction writers. Writing was considered the highest art form.

But we clever eggheads of today assume that the original writers had allowed fantasy stories to be inscribed on their clay tablets. I suggest that the ruler or chief priest at that time would never have allowed such misuse. It was truth that was conveyed. Why on earth did they then write, "And so, Gilgamesh was created by the Gods . . . two parts of him god-like, a third of him human"?

The gods of millennia ago were aliens. And they experimented with various creatures—including our ancestors. This does not categorically contradict evolution (whereby the question about the origin of chemical evolution is not the same as the one about the origin of biological evolution). We may well be products of biological evolution, but this evolution has repeatedly been interfered with. One might compare this to an apple tree. At some point, hundreds of thousands of years ago, there was something like a "primordial apple root" from which an apple developed in an evolutionary process. But then came man. And simply by grafting we changed the apple. Evolution and artificial mutation: these processes are not opposites.

Our geneticists will prove it. Man is not just the product of evolution. Bruce Fenton's book *Exogenesis* is a significant milestone in understanding our history. It should become a textbook at all schools.

—ERICH VON DÄNIKEN
April 2019
Author of *Chariots of the Gods* and
The Gods Never Left Us

PREFACE

When I was ten years old, I began to collect a set of forty cards that came free with my maternal grandmother's tea leaves. These cards were titled "Unexplained Mysteries of the World," and each detailed a bizarre phenomenon or some strange mystery from science or history. These cards provided my first encounters with cryptids, psychic powers, extraterrestrial craft, and lost civilizations.

My early encounters with the writing of the researcher Graham Hancock, and his book *Fingerprints of the Gods*, only increased my fascination with the puzzles implicit in the human story. His work offered tantalizing clues to a lost epoch in which humanity had acquired, and then lost, a great understanding of science and spirituality.

I was also fortunate to be introduced to the work of Erich von Däniken and his legendary *Chariots of the Gods*. This incredibly wide-ranging body of research identified streams of cultural evidence pointing to extraterrestrial contact with prehistoric human populations. This exploration opened my mind to the extraordinary possibility of past visitors arriving from the infinite cosmos where we are all space travelers.

During the thirty-two years that followed my first encounters with these mind-expanding subjects, I have dedicated much of my time to unraveling our complex history.

This has led me to explore ancient sites and enigmas on six of the seven continents.

My humble efforts have included internationally reported expeditions into the Amazon jungle and my leading of a Science Channel team into the Caucasus Mountains. It has been quite a journey to say the least and one I have been blessed and honored to share with my beloved wife and fellow researcher, Daniella.

Together we aim to carry the torch of greater understanding just a little bit further down the road, always remembering that we stand upon the shoulders of giants.

Our sincerest thanks are offered to all those fellow walkers on this path who blazed the trail ahead or extended their hand whenever we needed assistance.

INTRODUCTION

*A new scientific truth does not triumph by convincing
its opponents and making them see the light, but
rather because its opponents eventually die, and a new
generation grows up that is familiar with it.*

—MAX PLANCK, theoretical physicist

Two of the most significant questions for humanity are, How did we come into being, and are we alone in the universe?

Every living human being will likely wonder to themselves, at least once, whether intelligent life exists somewhere beyond this planet. It is a question that has played on the minds of leading scientists from many fields. These questions have also impacted the thoughts of philosophers and theologians. The exciting possibility of fellow beings out in the cosmos has driven artists and writers to create marvelous, fantastical depictions of possible alien creatures.

The mist-shrouded origins of our species and the creatures that preceded our arrival have led to a thousand different creation myths and dozens of religions. Scientists in various camps offer their own competing theories for the first emergence of life on Earth and the process of our evolution.

This book intends to definitively solve these mysteries once and for all—a grand endeavor, for sure—and you will be the ultimate judge as to whether it succeeds in these lofty aims.

This investigation presents the reader with stunning evidence that Earth has been known to extraterrestrial races right from the moment life appeared. Indeed, there is convincing evidence that an alien civilization seeded our world with DNA. Life here on Earth appeared as soon as the planet's crust solidified and even before the asteroid bombardments ended.

The delivery of life to our young world, known as panspermia or exogenesis, would have established a cosmic relationship with extraterrestrial progenitors from the very first moment. Though the scientific argument for life arriving from space is not new, evidence for panspermia has increased over time.

Assuming advanced beings were aware that our planet housed life from day one, then all the complex astronomical calculations in use today would tell us nothing about the chances of alien beings visiting Earth. We would instead need to consider whether a galactic intelligence had been quietly monitoring this world and taking an interest in the evolution of life on its surface.

As for better understanding the appearance of our own species . . . well, that is a subject in which we all share a vested interest. It is also a topic that has been rather poorly explained. Modern anthropological research has revealed that *Homo sapiens* have an incredibly mysterious evolutionary origin. Our closest living relatives are the chimpanzees, yet we are astonishingly unlike them and the other members of the great ape family.

While it is common to hear claims that we share 99 percent of our DNA with chimps, this has more recently proven to be a fundamentally flawed claim. When directly contrasted, the structure of the respective genomes has less than 95 percent direct concordance.[1] Millions of genetic differences exist between our chimp cousins and us, and many are far from trivial. Some smaller number of human genomic anomalies remain inexplicable without considering influences beyond the understood evolutionary forces.

Two highly polarized ideological camps have grown up around the deep and abiding mystery of human origins. Religious creationists stand on one side of the divide, positing divinely orchestrated intelligent design. Materialist reductionists are positioned on the other side of the intellectual chasm, claiming that humans are the product of random mutations and natural selection. Each group has the equivalent of a core doctrine replete with inexcusable bias and a tendency toward knee-jerk dismissal whenever faced with inconvenient facts.

The materialists and creationists have one essential thing in common: they are all incorrect in their understanding of the evolutionary emergence of *Homo sapiens.* This will become clear as we progress in our investigative journey.

You, the open-minded scholars of humanity, are about to walk with me through the deep impasse that separates these two monolithic origination narratives. We will explore astonishing scientific evidence that proves there is a superior "middle way."

This unique body of evidence that we are set to explore emerges from more than thirty years of investigative inquiry and a lifelong relationship with what I shall refer to as "the phenomena." The evidence brought to bear involves elements of both natural evolutionary processes and intelligent design; however, this is not divine intervention.

The culmination of this work is the conclusion that our ancient ancestors were the result of extraterrestrial genetic manipulation. This incursion, involving an already evolving hominin creature, occurred approximately 780,000 years ago. Clearly, this also answers the question of whether we are alone in the universe.

You will not be asked to take any of these bold claims purely on faith. We will explore genetic data and physical evidence that confirm the validity of this theory. You will be given access to not only particular DNA anomalies (fingerprints of the alien genetic engineers) but also material identified as wreckage from their interstellar vehicle.

There is perhaps no hope of convincing the ardent "pseudo-skeptics" who suffer from cognitive dissonance. Those persons driven by an overwhelming bias against new and controversial models will likely never even read this work. There will always be those persons unable to adapt to a paradigm change, defaulting instead to knee-jerk dismissal. It is, however, my opinion that we are on the verge of a completely new understanding of what it means to be "human."

We are not alone. We were never alone. We are children of the stars.

Consider here that humanity may have distant relatives of sorts existing somewhere beyond this planet. We will also explore the possibility that these highly advanced entities could potentially offer us assistance at a time when the fate of our ecological systems, and thus our species, hangs by the thinnest of threads. Our greatest hope for the future on Earth may lie with us claiming our place in a cosmos community.

Introduction

It is my opinion that humanity must choose to rise up and embrace the proffered contact process. We must engage with this alien intelligence waiting in the inky blackness of space or risk falling into the eternal darkness of extinction.

SECTION ONE

ALIEN CONTACT

All truth passes through three stages.
First, it is ridiculed. Second, it is violently opposed.
Third, it is accepted as being self-evident.

—ARTHUR SCHOPENHAUER, German philosopher

CHAPTER 1

AN ALIEN PARADIGM SHIFT

My personal belief is that there is very compelling
evidence that we may not be alone.

—LUIS ELIZONDO, former director, Advanced
Aviation Threat Identification Program

It's a rainy afternoon in South Wales, and I'm taking a break from writing about high strangeness to do the family shopping at the local supermarket. The supermarket seems an unlikely place for anything interesting to happen. The last thing I would expect while shopping is to stumble on anything relevant to my current research project, extraterrestrial intelligence (ETI). And yet, something catches my eye on the magazine shelf. I stop to look and see that it's the front cover of *National Geographic*.

The cover image is a radio telescope dish against the background of a star-filled night sky. Written in a huge capitalized white font are the words *WE ARE NOT ALONE*. I nod to myself and then point it out to my wife, Daniella. It's another confirmation of something we have already been discussing: we are in the early stages of an alien-related societal paradigm shift.

The cultural narrative on the existence of alien life and some form of intelligence beyond our world is rapidly shifting. NASA has long been out of the search for ETI, but recently this changed. It was announced that $10 million of their federal budget was mandated to be allocated to a search for alien *technosignatures,* meaning signatures of technology.[1] NASA quickly organized a conference in September 2018 at which scientists debated how best for NASA to rejoin the search for extraterrestrials. While the conference attendees discussed listening for radio signals or attempting to detect lasers, attendees also considered looking for technological artifacts and deliberately modified exoplanet environments.

While NASA has been out of the search for ETI, privately funded organizations have primarily been filling this gap. Most notable among the significant efforts to detect intelligence in the cosmos are those of the SETI Institute and more recently Breakthrough Initiatives. Founded in 1984, the SETI Institute currently represents the most prominent effort to actively seek signs of alien life in the cosmos. The SETI Institute is a privately funded organization that operates distinct from NASA but maintains good relations with that federally funded organization. The institute focuses resources on six divisions: astrobiology, astronomy and astrophysics, climate and biogeoscience, exoplanets, planetary exploration, and the search for extraterrestrial intelligence. There is little doubt that radio SETI is the best-known effort of the institution, with its primary focus on detection of artificially generated radio signals.

Despite decades of efforts and many interesting cosmological discoveries, the SETI Institute has failed to detect any signal that can be associated with the emissions of an advanced extraterrestrial civilization. The scientists in all the institute's various teams have collectively failed to find any sort of evidence that can be claimed to indicate the presence of life beyond our planet.

Breakthrough Initiatives began in 2015 with the financial support of Yuri Milner, an Israeli-Russian venture capitalist. There are four current projects. Breakthrough Listen is a $100 million funded program for astronomical observations of the nearest one million stars. Breakthrough Watch is a multimillion dollar effort to detect nearby Earth-like planets. Breakthrough Starshot is a $100 million engineering program aiming to put a fleet of unmanned probes into deep space. The Breakthrough Message project offers a $1 million prize for the design of a suitable signal that can be beamed into space.

So, what exactly is the basic model and assumption behind the search for extraterrestrial life? What do these scientists think about the chances of aliens existing and being detected?

The primary consideration for SETI (search for extraterrestrial intelligence) scientists is the sheer wealth of possible targets. In the average galaxy are an estimated one hundred million stars, and based on imaging carried out by the Hubble telescope, there are at least two trillion galaxies in the observable universe. Our brains are not evolved to process and visualize mathematical concepts on such a vast scale; however, it may be helpful to consider this approximates to about ten thousand stars for every grain of sand on Earth. This should boggle the mind of any thinking person.

Due to the incredible number of solar systems predicted to offer suitable environments for life—five hundred million in the Milky Way alone—most scientists share the belief that life must be out there somewhere. It is indeed not at all controversial to hold such a conviction, and most people expect life to exist in space. Glocalities conducted a survey with twenty-six thousand people living in twenty-six countries. Sixty-one percent of respondents believed alien life exists, and 47 percent thought that it could be intelligent.[2]

While astronomers and astrobiologists suspect intelligent aliens exist, some are left wondering why it is proving so hard to locate any of them. This perceived cosmic silence has led to suggestions that all other civilizations have gone extinct or that perhaps they are too far beyond our range of detection with current technologies.

Some academics have proposed somewhat esoteric-sounding hypotheses for the cosmic silence, such as humans being in a cosmic zoo of sorts, protected from direct interference by an unseen hand. Might Earth be a nature reserve where our primitive species can live life unmolested?

The lack of detection calls into question the methods being used and highlights the minimal extent of the search. We should also consider the limiting preconceptions and biases of the scientists working in the projects searching for evidence of life beyond Earth. You will rarely see something that you do not believe can exist, and it is difficult to encounter something you are not willing to find.

So far this search for alien life has involved an analysis of a region of the cosmos equivalent to just one bathtub of water taken from all the oceans of our planet. The astronomical exploration of distant environments has barely begun. It is clearly premature to speak of a cosmic silence or to suggest the uniqueness of terrestrial life. We should also keep in mind that leading physicists insist several higher dimensions that may be inhabited exist, and in some models, the universe is posited to be a highly advanced holographic simulation.

Apart from some efforts to seek out microbial life in our solar system, astronomers and astrobiologists almost exclusively focus on the possibility of life in far-off star systems. The search for intelligent life skips over our solar system entirely, highlighting the glaring and commonly held preconception that intelligent life must be far, far away. This is not a well-reasoned scientific position but merely a product of established dogma; there's no good reason to discount potential technosignatures in our own solar system. Things are indeed moving forward even if attitudes still need to change much further. Many years ago, when I was a child, any attempt to discuss aliens in polite society would almost certainly lead to dismissive remarks or silly jokes. While that has not entirely gone away, there is a noticeable sea change with a growing number of believers.

The younger members of society have been strongly influenced by alien-related television shows such as the History Channel's ever-popular flagship series *Ancient Aliens*. The series tackles the premise that ancient astronauts visited Earth in the remote past and interacted with our ancestors. This epic cosmic encounter allegedly had enormous influences on our cultural and religious development—as we would expect of such a meeting. It is undoubtedly true that indigenous cultures all around the globe openly claim a history of contact with cosmic spirits and sky gods. There is no shortage of abstract art and engraved mythology that seem to allude to this contact.

Ancient Aliens is mainly based on the research of the legendary Swiss author Erich von Däniken, most famous for his book series that began in 1968 with his best-selling *Chariots of the Gods*. This book and the many that followed in the series identified artifacts, structures, engravings, and oral history from around our planet that pointed to prehistoric contact between humans and advanced cosmic beings. Von Däniken essentially founded the ancient astronaut theory that has since gone on to be a focus for researchers around the globe.

Incidentally, just a few weeks after von Däniken's book was published, the ancient-aliens-themed blockbuster movie *2001: A Space Odyssey* hit cinemas. There is little doubt that 1968 was the year curiosity in possible ancient astronaut contact became a global phenomenon. Both the screenplay and the book also allude to the possibility that visitors from the stars meddled with human genetics.

Ancient Aliens has been running for more than a decade and is in its thirteenth season as of this writing. Though much of the evidence covered is subjective and open to other interpretations, some is incredibly compelling. There is substantial public acceptance of the central hypothesis due to the breadth of the highlighted data. How many cable shows are popular enough to survive twelve administrative review panels for potential renewal?

As popular as *Ancient Aliens* is, there is more to the growing public belief in alien contact with humanity than this favorite cable television show. We live in an era of social media, with thousands of YouTube channels, Facebook groups, Instagram feeds, and blogs dedicated to the subject of aliens and the unidentified flying objects suspected to be their vehicles: those chariots of the alien gods.

Hundreds of thousands of websites have at some stage covered the topic of extraterrestrials visiting Earth. Even mainstream media is forced to publish content on this subject due to the overwhelming popularity. Aliens are no longer limited to outer space and a few B movies; they permeate our global culture.

To highlight the shift in beliefs, consider the Economist/ YouGov poll on popular beliefs published in October 2018. This survey revealed that around 35 percent of US citizens believe extraterrestrials have at some time landed on Earth.[3] Meanwhile, a related Slashdot survey of more than thirteen thousand international respondents revealed that there was a 36 percent acceptance rate of visitation by intelligent extraterrestrial life-forms.[4] The number of alien contact believers, as indicated by such surveys, has been climbing year after year.

When I began researching ancient mysteries almost thirty years ago, it would have been unimaginable that the day was coming when a third of people would believe advanced aliens had visited Earth. The person running such a survey would have been considered a lunatic for even asking these questions. The shift in our collective cultural narrative is starkly apparent, and I predict that it will inevitably continue.

There is little doubt that a significant part of the community of contact believers include unidentified flying objects (UFOs) as part of the evidence supporting their position. While it is true that people often mistake natural or human phenomena for something more mysterious, every year thousands of genuinely bizarre sightings occur. Among the estimated 5 percent of UFOs considered truly abnormal are encounters with intelligently controlled structured vehicles incorporating a technology beyond human comprehension.[5] It is this 5 percent of encounters that we discuss in this book; the other 95 percent with reasonable explanations are of no interest here.

There are so many mind-blowing encounters between humans and UFOs—or what I prefer to call anomalous aerial phenomena (AAP)—that to do that subject justice requires an entire narrowly focused book. Many books tackle people's AAP encounters, so I'll merely share some of our own personal experiences of this type.

While I have had several sightings of AAP, one stands out in my mind. It was 1996, and I was eighteen years old. My friends and I were returning to Stroud from a party in Malmsbury (Gloucestershire, UK). As five of us young men drove back through the dark and empty country lanes, we noticed a white light moving erratically in the sky. This prompted us to stop the car and make some more focused observations.

While the light above us was itself not all that odd, merely a steady white point of luminosity, whatever it was emanating from behaved most astonishingly. One moment it would be flying along to the left, then it would vanish and reappear moving toward the right. Repeatedly the light would pop out of visibility and instantaneously appear again in a distant part of the night sky. Each time it became visible, once again it would be moving in a new direction, whether left, right, up, or down.

I am certainly not an authority in aviation and do not pretend to have access to secret military projects. I can't conclusively say that we were not witnessing an air force test vehicle. However, I grew up near an air force base and could readily discount jets and helicopters.

Whatever the object was, it was able to teleport. It is difficult to believe that there was anything that advanced in the military inventory back in the 1990s. Even if there were, it would raise questions as to how such advanced capabilities had been acquired. In my estimation it was either alien in nature or the Royal Air Force (RAF) had been gifted teleportation technology by benevolent star beings.

Incidentally, the alleged deep state whistle-blower Bob Lazar claims that he worked on recovered alien crafts at a facility called S4 near Groom Lake, Nevada. On one occasion he brought UFO researcher John Lear to witness one of the secret aircraft being tested. The description is of a light jumping between points in the sky. The report of the drive system purportedly involves claimed gravity-wave amplification that pulls your target location to the ship. When the drive is turned off, the position instantly snaps back, taking the craft with it.

Daniella has witnessed a startling example of an anomalous aerial vehicle (AAV). The experience had a profound impact on her and remains the most vivid encounter she has had with something resembling an advanced technology from beyond this world.

Daniella's encounter with the strange aerial craft happened in 1999. In late evening Daniella drove with her father between downtown Sydney and the international airport. They saw that cars ahead were slowing down, as if there had been an accident. They slowed down and then noticed people were getting out of their vehicles and looking up at the sky. They stopped and did the same thing.

Looking toward the airport, Daniella and her father noticed that immediately above the control tower, three triangular craft were hovering in a tight triangle formation. Each aircraft had a white light at the end of its three points; another situated in the central area slowly pulsed on and off. After about five minutes the craft suddenly shot away from each other in separate directions.

Daniella and her dad got back into the car and drove into the nearby bypass tunnel. Upon exiting, they noticed one of the three objects was now above their vehicle. They followed the Grand Parade to Brighton-le-Sands, a small beachside suburb, and then continued driving for about fifteen minutes. The craft kept close, always about 150 to three hundred feet above them. It eventually made a nearer approach; trees lining the road seemed to keep it limited to their topmost heights. After the object moved toward them, they noticed that the car radio began to make unusual noises. The car's engine also seemed to be affected by the craft and sounded as if it was struggling. Fearing the car might stall and break down, Daniella told her dad to head to a nearby McDonald's, where more people would be around. It was only at this stage that the craft began to lift away vertically, before shooting off at a breakneck speed.

It was only after the strange triangle vanished that her father admitted that he had seen unmanned aerial vehicles (UAVs) and AAP when he was just a young man in his country of origin, Ecuador. On one such occasion, he was among a crowd that witnessed a strange circular craft hovering stationary high above the cathedral in the city center of Ambato.

The other instances of AAP my father-in-law experienced all occurred while he was working in the Ecuadorian Amazon jungles. Sometimes while he was in the forest at night, strange glowing orbs would appear. On at least one occasion the luminous spheres pursued him at high speed as he attempted to flee in his jeep. Glowing orbs are among the most common types of AAP.

Don Donderi, a retired McGill professor of psychology, has studied the phenomena for more than fifty years. He now teaches a course called UFOs: History and Reality. Following a recent encounter involving two commercial planes and a fast-moving luminous AAP, Donderi was asked for his comments. He suggested the observations might be of an extraterrestrial vehicle, adding, "People have close encounters of the second kind. Pilots have reported seeing vehicles within 100 yards of them. They see an actual shape, an object suspended in the sky, hovering over them, with windows, surrounded by a luminous glow—and then it moves off abruptly."[6]

Anecdotal accounts of people interacting with UAVs and AAP number beyond counting. It was once easy for skeptics to dismiss such things as being misidentification of normal aircraft or delusion on the part of the witness, but a number of events have made it far more difficult for narrow-minded debunkers.

CHAPTER 2

ANOMALOUS AERIAL
PHENOMENA

These aircraft—we'll call them aircraft—are
displaying characteristics that are not currently
within the US inventory nor in any foreign
inventory that we are aware of.

—LUIS ELIZONDO, To the Stars
Academy of Arts and Science (TTSA)

In late 2017, an astonishing story appeared across various major news platforms around the globe. It was revealed that the US military, specifically the Department of Defense (DOD), had been running a secretive AAP-focused project.[1] The official name of this project was the Advanced Aviation Threat Identification Program (AATIP). Journalists had interviewed Luis Elizondo, the former head of operations at AATIP and a career intelligence officer and microbiologist, who announced that he had recently stepped down from his covert DOD position.

Elizondo has since explained two significant frustrations that drove his decision to retire. The first was the unnecessarily secretive nature of the project. The second was more perplexing, as it centered upon a strong pushback from senior Pentagon officials. It seems that some senior staff believed AAP might be demonic or angelic in nature and were best left alone. Elizondo, however, has stated that his project identified compelling evidence of non-terrestrial technologies associated with some AAP moving freely through our airspace.

It is rather astonishing to hear that senior US intelligence officials wanted to close a secret AAP research program on the grounds of religious concerns. Nick Pope, former AAP investigator for Britain's Ministry of Defence, has since confirmed that religious fears were similarly present among UK brass.[2] In the corridors of power, strange lights in the sky are believed by some to represent messengers of the gods. This spiritual revelation is perhaps the only thing stranger than learning that aliens might be visiting our planet.

Since leaving AATIP, Elizondo has joined a privately run multimedia organization called To the Stars Academy of Arts and Science (TTSA). The company was founded by multimillionaire punk-rock star Tom DeLonge, formerly of Blink-182. TTSA is split into three divisions: media, aerospace, and science. Fortunately for my investigations, a helpful new introduction video was recently added to the TTSA website. In this slick promotional video, Tom DeLonge reveals that his organization has more in mind than just publishing books and producing sci-fi movies—a hell of a lot more.

DeLonge explains that during his research into various AAP-related topics, he recognized that there were people in government positions who might want to engage the public on controversial scientific subjects that have become stigmatized. There did not seem to be any obvious mechanism for these people to achieve such an aim and so DeLonge created TTSA as a platform they could use.

Through a series of meetings, he made contact with several interested individuals from the Central Intelligence Agency (CIA), the DOD, and the secretive aerospace corporation Lockheed Martin Skunk Works. The people he networked with were purportedly all keen to leave a positive legacy that would benefit the world and be involved in shifting humanity onto a better path.

Among the stated TTSA objectives is the development of advanced propulsion systems based on pulsed light and antigravity engines that bend the fabric of space-time. The science division is supposedly bringing us an artificial intelligence (AI)–driven database full of unexplained phenomena. Details of their ongoing analysis of exotic materials allegedly recovered from UAVs are also expected.[3] Anyone intrigued by this will be interested to know that the TTSA team are also the subject of a reality television show on the History Channel. Surely, watching former government intelligence agents investigating pieces of alien spacecraft will be a welcome change from seeing vacuous celebrities moaning about their pampered lives.

DeLonge has recently claimed that TTSA has partnered with groups inside the DOD and the wider intelligence community. Considering the former establishment careers of his team members, it is not hard to believe his claims. The TTSA team has already helped to bring mainstream media interest to declassified military videos of AAP intercepts involving US fighter craft (gun camera footage). The videos associated with TTSA reveal the extraordinary capabilities of the mysterious objects encountered by US fighter pilots. We can see objects without wings, propellers, or any visible propulsion systems performing maneuvers that should technically result in fatally strong g-forces. One of the recorded objects has been referred to as a forty-foot-long "tic-tac." At the 2019 Scientific Conference on Anomalous Aerospace Phenomena, Luis Elizondo said, "These things are performing hypersonic velocity in some cases. They have been officially clocked at over 13,000 mph. Unofficially, much, much faster. And by the way, these are through military capabilities. Okay? Not grandma saw some lights in the backyard."[4]

The TTSA team has suggested that some of the AAP may represent a potential military threat and as such should be an intelligence-gathering priority. This very strong stance is certainly not entirely unfounded. Apart from the inability of advanced terrestrial aircraft to even keep up with these things, there have been several incidents involving AAP and malfunctioning nuclear weapons. Military observers have sighted strange objects hovering above nuclear weapons facilities, which have then spontaneously gone offline. Nuclear missiles are not something we want to fall under the control of an entirely mysterious force with unknown intentions.

One example of the many nuclear-related incidences was revealed by Captain Robert Salas. On a fateful day in March 1967, a strange, saucer-shaped craft hovered near the Malmstrom Air Force Base, where he was stationed. At the same moment that the object hovered above the facility, several of the nuclear missiles went offline. Captain Salas was contacted shortly afterward by one of the security-gate officers. The panicked solider reported a terrifying confrontation with a pulsating red orb. Soon after this Salas learned that ten missiles had similarly deactivated at another nearby installation.[5]

The reporting of interactions between military personnel and anomalous aerial vehicles is indeed not something new. A significant number of strange encounters between mysterious glowing spheres (usually orange or red) and both Allied and Nazi aircraft occurred during World War II. Pilots were often followed by the peculiar spheres, even during evasive maneuvers. Some of these orbs appeared on military radar, suggesting they were at least partially physical and not reducible to visual anomalies. Pilots are considered expert observers of the sky, well used to the full range of known aerial phenomena, from strange weather and reflective clouds to blimps and foreign aircraft. When a pilot reports an unknown object in the sky, such accounts should rightly provoke serious attention.

Emeritus professor Peter Sturrock of Stanford University has been quite direct in his opinion that radar represents compelling physical evidence for the objective reality of UAVs. In 1942, Sturrock interrupted his studies to help in the war effort and joined the Telecommunications Research Establishment (later renamed the Royal Radar Establishment), where he assisted in the development of radar systems. As Sturrock states, when it comes to detection of AAP, "Yes—radar is physical evidence."[6]

I witnessed a cluster of these strange orange orbs in 2002. While watching a planetary alignment from my back garden, I observed a dozen orange orbs flying in a loose formation high above me. What really grabbed me was the astonishing speed at which they traveled, completing the journey from one horizon to the other in less than a minute. I reported my encounter to the press, which somehow led to it appearing not only in a local newspaper but also as a small feature in the UK's (now defunct) *UFO Magazine*.

One common claim is that glowing orbs such as those highlighted already are merely examples of *ball lightning*. This may at first sound as if the mystery is solved, but when you dig a little deeper, it becomes evident that ball lightning remains an entirely anomalous phenomenon. The only thing that can be said for certain about this strange type of AAP is that it is spherical and doesn't match the scientific definition of lightning. Most scientists accept the existence of ball lightning–related phenomena simply due to the incredible volume of reports stretching right back to the ancient Greeks. Statistical analysis carried out by J. R. McNally in 1960 revealed that about 5 percent of the global population has encountered this type of spherical AAP.[7]

The strange glowing spheres can range in size (most common is soccer ball–sized), and color varies among red, orange, blue, and white. These luminous balls often appear in relative proximity to a thunderstorm: sometimes a little before, during, or a while after. According to A. I. Grigoriev, a researcher who analyzed more than ten thousand cases of suspected ball lightning, the duration of the phenomena depends mostly on the observed size and brilliance. The larger and dimmer the ball, the longer it remains stable, sometimes persisting for many minutes.[8]

The most common explanation for these spherical AAP is that they are some type of plasma structure. Plasma is the fourth state of matter, hot ionized gas with balanced ions and electrons. However, many of the reported observations make this somewhat unlikely. Another offered explanation has focused on maser effects resulting from microwave amplification by stimulated emission of radiation. This provides a better fit but still fails to answer all the mysteries of what causes the initial formation and behavior of the spheres, especially when they appear without any storm having begun and no lightning strikes.

What makes this phenomenon especially baffling is that not only can it appear suddenly from nowhere and vanish much the same way but at other times the movement seems to be intelligently directed. These luminous orbs sometimes enter buildings by coming down the chimney or up a drain and then float around in front of people. Sometimes they just vanish, while in other instances they pass through the glass of a closed window. There are accounts of these orbs splitting into two, materializing and dematerializing with associated enormous explosive booms and leaving burned-out electrical equipment in their wake. Despite being hypothesized as high energy events, the balls can "explode" at proximity to a person without so much as singeing an eyebrow.

There is incredible overlap between many of the observations associated with so-called ball lightning and other AAP that are observed without any connection to thunderstorms. Orbs meeting the same description have been witnessed coming out of large, structured UAVs, and they seem to behave like reconnaissance drones.

As it stands, science does not know what causes and directs these phenomena, and they can't be re-created in a lab. It seems to me a straightforward academic rule is at play here: when a glowing orb is observed in proximity to a thunderstorm, it's written off as ball lightning (which is unexplained), and if observed distinct from any storm activity, it falls into the realm of fantastical delusions. That is not how objective scientific analysis is supposed to work!

Sightings of strange flying objects continued unabated after the end of World War II. On June 24, 1947, private pilot Kenneth Arnold encountered a string of nine shiny objects flying past Mount Rainier at speeds estimated to be higher than twelve hundred miles an hour.[9] News coverage of the event used the now iconic term *flying saucers*, despite the fact that Arnold only suggested the objects skipped along like saucers skimming across the water.

Strangely enough, AAP began to regularly manifest as disc-shaped objects after news media wrongly reported on Kenneth Arnold's sighting. The associated phenomenon seemingly obligingly adapted itself to the new popular cultural narrative. A few weeks after Arnold's encounter there were media reports of a downed flying saucer at Roswell, New Mexico. The Roswell crash is now a central feature in UFO lore and has made the city a place of pilgrimage for believers. Today, Roswell even has its own local UFO museum and research center.

If the witness accounts and claims from military insiders are based in truth, the crashed alien vehicle, along with the bodies of its crew, was recovered in a secret military operation. Many researchers claim technology from the Roswell craft was reverse-engineered and used to improve existing military hardware. You won't be shocked to hear that the US government does not endorse such a story and prefers the version involving a weather balloon brought down by storm activity (perhaps ball lightning?).

From the Foo Fighters of WWII onward, there have continued to be reports of AAP coming from pilots, including those in commercial aviation. We must consider here that commercial pilots typically consider it risky to report AAP or UAVs. Few pilots want to risk being deemed unfit to fly, and as such, any reports shared by pilots should be taken very seriously indeed.

The astonishing number of AAP sightings involving people from all walks of life has led to enormous public interest in the subject. While not everyone believes strange lights in our skies need be linked to alien visitation, a significant number of people think that is precisely the case. With a growing level of military acknowledgment that AAP and UAVs are penetrating controlled airspace comes greater public acceptance. As psychologist Don Donderi, PhD, explains, humans often find it most comfortable to convince themselves there is no evidence of strange phenomena. They usually prefer to consider those who accept the existence of ETs as being mentally ill or seekers of personal gain. "If everyone realizes we're being surveilled by extra-terrestrials who have better machinery than we do, we have a potential problem," says Donderi. "But any sensible person will say the first step in dealing with any problem is admitting it exists."[10]

It may seem somewhat ironic that, despite broad acceptance of strange forces and alien visitors among senior military officials and their contracted scientists, there remains widespread dismissal in key academic fields. The academics involved with official efforts in the search for extraterrestrial intelligence (ETI) remain overwhelmingly hostile toward the inclusion of AAP or UAVs in their parameters, let alone anything hinting at psychical or spiritual phenomena.

To better understand why there is such a different point of view held by SETI researchers, we need to explore their limiting prejudices with respect to alien life and the reductive filters they employ when looking for acceptable evidence. Let's start with a look at the scientific method being used.

The scientific method is an empirical structure for acquiring knowledge employing careful repeated observations. Rigorous skepticism is applied to that which is observed. It's an understood fact that observers' mental assumptions can distort the interpretation of their views. Once enough inspections have been carried out, hypotheses are formulated. A scientific hypothesis is an informed conjecture based on data acquired while attempting to answer the proposed question. Scientists test hypotheses through suitable experiments or studies. One fixed condition is that any scientific theory must be falsifiable; that is, there must be the possibility of an outcome from the investigations that conflicts with predictions.

Without falsifiability, the hypothesis cannot be meaningfully tested. An example of an open-ended assumption is the suggestion that God created the universe. Nobody has come up with any way to design a structured experiment that could discount this as a possibility—meaning it is not a falsifiable hypothesis.

In this methodology we hit on some of the problems that have put SETI scientists off from the consideration of AAP, UAVs, and the more difficult encounters with what seem to be alien beings. It's tough to construct a falsifiable hypothesis involving a fleeting phenomenon that does not reliably repeat. How do scientists obtain multiple observations and conduct experiments if their target appears briefly just once at the location and then never again? Conceiving of experiments that will falsify the hypothesis that AAP and UAVs are manifestations of an intelligent alien civilization is incredibly challenging. The starting point is to discount all known natural and artificial phenomena, which assumedly has already occurred in these cases, but that does not preclude unknown natural events or secret military technologies. As the scientists have extreme uncertainty as to how an advanced intelligence might manifest and no sample alien vehicles, they have an open-ended potential list and nothing to use as a suitable reference. Is a glowing orb that skips around the sky an alien ship or a yet-to-be-understood natural energy phenomena?

This is one of the primary reasons why SETI scientists have distanced themselves from AAP. Detailed witness statements are feeble evidence for academics working in the hard sciences, and though there is a wealth of photographs of lights in the sky, there is not much they can do with such data, even if they find it intriguing. Some tangible evidence is associated with AAP and UAVs, but it is sparse and difficult to acquire.

We should remember that there are also strong biases at work. As previously mentioned, most space scientists believe the distances between stars make a visitation to Earth almost impossible. This is a limiting bias that we will soon show to be unfounded, but it continues to influence SETI scientists in their thinking.

To be clear, I am not saying it is impossible to formulate useful scientific research programs that could investigate AAP. It might even be possible for scientists to identify some of the aerial phenomena as being controlled by an unknown intelligence, at the least. However, from a SETI perspective, I imagine this identification process is something they feel could be better done by other parties.

Keep in mind that SETI scientists, whether with NASA, the European Space Agency (ESA), or the SETI Institute, don't have access to jet fighters that can pursue UAPs or the types of military surveillance equipment that can readily detect, track, and analyze fast-moving AAP. They are not necessarily well equipped to investigate all kinds of AAP and UAVs even if they wanted to do so (which they clearly don't).

One thing to clarify here is that astronomers do sometimes detect these AAP. In an article for a popular science website, Kevin Knuth, an associate professor of physics, highlighted a 1977 survey of 2,611 astronomers. Astrophysics professor Peter Sturrock found that, of the 1,356 respondents to his survey, 4.6 percent had observed inexplicable aerial phenomena. About 80 percent of the astronomers who responded indicated a willingness to help investigate AAP were there some organized way for them to participate. Knuth himself believes that "there is a great deal of evidence that a small percentage of these UFO sightings are unidentified structured craft exhibiting flight capabilities beyond any known human technology."[11]

If the US military were to officially confirm to NASA, SETI, and Breakthrough Initiatives that they had identified alien vehicles or retrieved physical material, this would undoubtedly be a game changer. There would no longer be any way for SETI programs to step back from the matter of AAP and UAVs. It would also effectively conclude the search for signs of extraterrestrial intelligence and take scientists to the post-detection stage of an investigation. For now, SETI programs have a structure in place that the scientists are familiar with and feel confident is appropriate. Researchers seemingly believe that they can remain within the parameters of the scientific method and "eventually" detect signs of alien life. Whether these beliefs and the choice of direction are well founded remains a matter of considerable debate.

To some degree, that debate is at least starting to occur. A March 2018 white paper published by Silvano Colombano, a scientist at the NASA Ames Research Center in California, argues that the scientific community should "consider the UFO phenomenon worthy of study."[12] Colombano also suggests that academics might engage in "speculative physics" with some "willingness to stretch possibilities as to the nature of space-time and energy."[13] As Colombano works for the Intelligent Systems Division, it is perhaps no surprise that he suspects ETI might be in a technological form such as extremely small superintelligence, something akin to advanced AI nanobot probes.

Colombano argues that it is time to rethink limiting assumptions such as whether aliens could acquire interstellar modes of travel. Even without faster-than-light propulsion systems, aliens might travel to new stars employing multigenerational missions, use suspended animation, or merely send out clouds of long-lived robotic probes. Colombano takes issue with the likelihood of radio waves being used by more advanced civilizations and is doubtful whether they would even be distinguishable from random noise. Two of his biggest complaints are (1) the assumption that life would be carbon based and biological and (2) the dogmatic belief that our planet has never been visited, despite the wealth of AAP reports.

Colombano suggests using big data analysis techniques to sift through the 130,000 pages of declassified US Air Force documents, the National UFO Reporting Center Database, and several other international information storage systems. While he considers it likely most of the stored reports would be "noise," he suspects there might be a core "signal" hidden within that could challenge existing negative presuppositions.[14]

The lack of serious academic interest in UAPs as potential signs of alien intelligence is not, then, due to any widespread lack of belief in extraterrestrial life. The scientific blind spot emerges from a combination of failing to sort through the best evidence and a need to dispel the assumption that life must be isolated to some distant star system. This ill-informed and dogmatic position adopted by SETI researchers leaves them to assume AAP must be confused observations of natural phenomena and human-engineered objects such as advanced secret military planes.

We currently have high-level military recognizing a possible extraterrestrial or interdimensional visitation.

Intelligence experts are worried about alien invaders wresting control of our nuclear weapons. Meanwhile, the SETI community remains ambivalent and focuses on detecting microbes in the atmospheres of distant exoplanets.

At least now we have an understanding of why this bizarre situation exists and what exactly is needed to change the state of play. Ideally, we want to move beyond AAP photographs or witness accounts. For this to happen, we need physical evidence that is tangible and objective and that compels consideration of intelligent extraterrestrial involvement. What evidence would indicate to scientists that an alien civilization has been, or is currently, operating within the vicinity of this planet?

Professor Paul Davies is perhaps the best-known SETI astrobiologist. He also happens to be a theoretical physicist. Davies is on the SETI Post-Detection Taskgroup team. This makes Davies perhaps the best person to instruct us on what type of alien evidence is needed. Davies has openly discussed the possibility that advanced ETI might have operated in the Sol system in the remote past, perhaps millions of years ago. The universe is indeed old enough, at 13.7 billion years, to allow for any early life-forms to have reached Earth from nearby stars even with sub-lightspeed craft.

When asked about possible long-lasting technosignatures that scientists could seek out in our solar system, Davies has a few suggestions to offer. He explains that any oddly chopped-up asteroids and other signs of mining, or nuclear waste, would act as extremely long-lasting signatures. Davies expresses a personal draw toward the possibility an ETI might have used biotechnologies and modified the genome of organisms on Earth. Any genetic modifications could potentially leave extremely long duration traces even if unintended. If aliens wanted to deliberately leave a calling card, there are ways they could ensure a near-eternal fingerprint in the genome.

As we will discover a little later, traces of alien biotechnologies and evidence of their interstellar vehicles exist but have previously gone unrecognized. Somewhat ironically, Davies himself notes that, due to scientists having little idea about the nature of alien civilizations, relevant evidence could already be stored among the vast amounts of genomic data, astronomical data, climatic data, and particle physics data. This is absolutely the case, as we uncovered during our research process.

Davies also clarifies that, with respect to radio SETI, it is highly unlikely a radio-astronomer looking for a message beamed from space will be the person that first discovers a cosmic intelligence. Davies explains, "It's more likely to come from someone who has no interest in SETI, sees something they don't understand that over time won't go away, and other people will dismiss it until it forces itself on the community." [15]

You have heard it straight from the horse's mouth: the most likely detection scenario doesn't involve a radio-astronomer. Instead it will likely be someone outside of the field entirely—perhaps some ancient-mysteries researcher busy investigating human origins might just stumble on the SETI holy grail.

CHAPTER 3

STRANGE ENCOUNTERS

*Yes, it's both. It's both literally, physically
happening to a degree; and it's also some kind of
psychological, spiritual experience occurring and
originating perhaps in another dimension.*

—DR. JOHN MACK, psychiatrist

Sightings of AAP and UAVs are peculiar enough, though
the associated high strangeness is certainly not limited to our skies. There has been a steady stream of claims
involving direct interactions between people and what
seems to be an ETI.

One of the most subtle anomalous experiences linked to
AAP is the claim that the object is somehow aware of the
witness. In some instances, the witness is even able to influence the phenomena. People have claimed to successfully
call the AAP to appear with their willpower alone. Their
thinking about the desire for communication has prompted
lights to flash on and off as if in response to the psychic
request. This slew of supernatural strangeness has led to a
practice known as the CE-5 initiative.

CE-5 is mostly a result of efforts by well-known AAP
researcher Dr. Steven Greer. Many people know Greer from

his documentary *Sirius Disclosure.* Greer's CE-5 protocol purportedly involves deliberate bilateral communication between humans and the intelligence associated with the AAP. In some cases, those involved report psychically receiving "downloads" of information from the anomalous objects hovering above them. (For more information, the website of Greer's Centre for the Study of Extraterrestrial Intelligence [CSETI] includes details on how to develop such contacts.)

Without a doubt the most powerful AAP-linked phenomenon is the so-called *alien abduction experience.* Although there is considerable variation across the accounts, we can offer a general description of such an event. Typically, the individual involved will have seen some form of AAP previously, often shortly before the abduction experience. Often enough the AAP is observed hovering above their home. The person typically wakes up in bed unable to move, as with sleep paralysis, and then notices strange beings in their bedroom. These entities (often short gray humanoids with swollen heads and bulbous eyes) then levitate them from their bed and out of their home into a waiting aerial vehicle. In many of these cases, the abductee reports passing straight through a closed window or even the bedroom wall.

Alien abductees sometimes remember the complete event upon waking, but in other instances they may have only a partial recall. Sometimes all the individual has is a strong sense that something strange has happened. In many cases, the person starts to have strange recurrent nightmares and then decides to seek a hypnotic regression therapist. Hypnotic regression can be a useful tool for recovering suppressed memories. Such sessions often bring about near complete recall of forgotten events.

One of the most notable investigators of these experiences was Dr. John Mack. Mack was a Pulitzer Prize–winning research psychiatrist who worked at Harvard University. He had been a researcher of dreams, nightmares, and adolescent suicide, but he began to study people claiming to recall an interaction with alien entities. Even though he had the best of credentials, his colleagues and even the university itself turned on him. The academic persecution of Mack began when he revealed that he believed the people involved were sane and that the experiences genuine, whether caused by aliens or some other unknown factor. This broke the unspoken academic rule that such strange phenomena must always be considered little more than fanciful nonsense.[1]

More recent investigations by psychologists have substantiated that overwhelmingly the people reporting abduction events are free of any apparent mental illness. Whatever is causing the phenomena is not merely a matter of apparent mental aberration and delusion. Professor Graham Davey, a psychologist at the University of Sussex, notes that work carried out by Professor Rich McNally and his fellow researchers at Harvard University indicated insanity was not part of the profile for interviewed experiencers.

McNally's team spent more than ten years researching the psychology of alien abductees. They eventually collated a list of common traits:[2]

1. Regularly experiencing sleep paralysis and hallucinations when awakening.

2. High levels of "absorption," a susceptibility to hypnosis and suggestion.

3. New Age beliefs.

4. A familiarity with the cultural narrative of alien abduction.

5. The tendency to recall false memories.

It may be tempting to see this as a strong indication that these people, while sane, are predisposed to unusual imaginary experiences and misinterpretation of more mundane events. Davey points out that because these people are being assessed after the event, we can't know whether the traits invoked the experiences or emerged from them.[3]

Another one of the most notable investigators of these experiences is David Jacobs, a retired professor of history formerly at Temple University. Jacobs has conducted well over one thousand regressions of alleged abductees himself and collated hundreds more from other independent regression sessions. He is convinced of the reality of physical events behind many of the memories, though he is open about the fact that secondhand regression reports of recovered memories, often from amateur hypnotherapists, are about the weakest form of evidence he can imagine. The sheer volume of such reports is, however, enough to call for the matter to be examined more closely.[4]

There are legitimate criticisms of the reliance on hypnotism in alien abduction accounts. It is possible for an overly eager therapist to accidentally prompt false memories. Such concern is merited, but we should keep in mind that most of these people sought out a regression session only because they already had fragments of memory that suggested an abduction had occurred.

A great many alien abductees have more than just memories. One alien abductee experiencer I know, Terry Lovelace, has been able to confirm the presence of a strange metal implant near his knee. X-ray images showed a small device with a metallic coil protruding from it. The object was strange enough in itself, but expert analysis revealed that there was no evidence of a healed entry wound. Doctors and radiologists were left baffled as to how the anomalous object could end up deep in his leg without damaging any of the tissue above.

Lovelace is the author of the bestselling book *Incident at Devil's Den*, in which he tells his personal story of multiple abductions and encounters with anomalous aerial vehicles. Many of his experiences occurred during his period of military service with the US Air Force. After one especially bizarre encounter, which left Lovelace and a fellow officer highly radioactive, he was detained and questioned by the Air Force Office of Secret Investigations (AFOSI). His experiences and evidence strongly support a reality in which people are physically taken by real nonhuman beings. Perhaps more remarkable is that the AFOSI had a team specifically tasked to investigate alien abductions involving military personnel!

During a later encounter with one of the nonhuman beings, Lovelace was informed that, due to his efforts to reveal his interactions, the object was being reclaimed. In a subsequent X-ray examination, the implant had indeed vanished.[5]

Terry Lovelace is far from alone in having been left with physical effects from his abductions. There are many accounts of abductees waking up with blood on their sheets from mysterious wounds, including surgical cuts, scoop marks, and even carved geometric shapes. In a small number of cases abductees have been returned to locations outside their homes, or with their clothes strangely rearranged, as though haphazardly put back on by someone unfamiliar with human clothing.

Medical procedures related to the reproductive system are among the most recurrent themes found in alien abduction memories. Men typically report machines that extract semen samples, and women report having eggs harvested.

Horrifyingly, female abductees claim to have embryos implanted in their wombs and return to their normal lives unexplainably pregnant. Fetuses relating to an abduction event tend to disappear from the womb at around three months. This period meshes closely with the biological fact that an abnormal fetus will usually be spontaneously aborted by the reproductive system before the end of the first trimester. At least on the face of it, the impression is that the entities recover the fetus just before the body's rejection. These female experiencers, during a later abduction event, are presented with a strange-looking human-alien hybrid child that they are informed (by telepathy) has been created from their genetic material.

The scientific community understandably struggles with claims of alien abduction and hybrid children. It is indeed a lot to take in, and the evidence is mind blowing. However, there must be a reason for thousands of people reporting almost identical occurrences of this type. There is a need for an open-minded rigorous investigation by suitably skilled researchers. I tend toward the position that some of these abductions are physical, as supported by tangible traces. Many of these events implicate altered states of consciousness. In both cases, there are potential paths of scientific investigation, which must be explored. Whatever the beliefs of scientists, they must acknowledge there are thousands of people left psychologically injured by the vivid and horrifying memories of whatever this phenomenon may be.

There is some degree of overlap between many abduction experiences and sleep disorders affecting REM (rapid eye movement) sleep, which is typically when dream states occur. REM intrusion involves the brain producing vivid dreamlike imagery while someone is awake. If this happens as we start the sleep cycle, it is referred to as hypnagogic;

if it happens as we are waking, then hypnopompic. There is also a common condition known as sleep paralysis, in which the experiencer finds themselves awake but unable to move more than their eyes. Sleep paralysis often comes replete with a terrifying sense of an immediate threat.

When sleep paralysis and REM intrusion are combined, they can indeed produce some vivid and bizarre experiences that are incredibly frightening. The more knowledgeable skeptics of alien abduction phenomena often highlight this as the cause of such reports.

The trouble with positing sleep paralysis with REM intrusion as causal for alien abductions is twofold: First, it would not be expected to prompt the same dream imagery for thousands of individuals. Why is it so often there is an experience of abduction by little bug-eyed gray men keen on extracting reproductive materials? Second, we would be attempting to solve one mystery by ascribing it to yet another. Researchers do not understand why this anomalous malfunction of brain activity happens. It reminds us of the ball lightning explanation for spherical AAP.

Simply putting names on things does not explain them. It's just an example of scientists kicking the can down the road. We have no idea how an alien technology might work and whether sleep paralysis with REM intrusion is not itself being deliberately triggered by an external intelligence. Perhaps the entities are keen to experiment on how humans would react in a situation in which they were physically abducted and experimented on. Such manipulation of human consciousness might be used as a precursor to selecting victims for subsequent phases of the alien's biological experiment. This would make the non-physical abduction experience an aspect of a fully immersive virtual-reality technology program.

Vast numbers of people are convinced that the astonishingly high number of AAP sightings and nocturnal abduction reports together represent compelling evidence of alien interaction with humanity. We can hardly blame them: it is the most obvious conclusion to leap to, no matter how intrinsically bizarre and problematic.

Daniella and I are among those people impacted by alien abduction experiences. We have also experienced a wide range of seemingly related anomalous terrestrial phenomena (ATP). My first relevant experiences occurred in the form of recurrent vivid nightmares. As a very young child, I would find myself dreaming that I was on a metal table surrounded by strange humanoid entities. One of them reminded me of the *Star Wars* character Chewbacca and another of the vampire Count Dracula. I never thought much about why I was there, but one thing that stood out at the time was seeing the skin of one of the beings splitting open, allowing thick slimy red "blood" to slowly ooze out. I certainly did not leap to the assumption that this was an alien abduction. As a young child, I had never heard anything about people being experimented on by aliens. I assumed the whole thing was just a horrible dream. I used to suffer regular nose bleeds when I was young, which is supposedly common in alien abductees, but these were not necessarily on days following the strange experiences. There is nothing I could call compelling physical evidence that aliens were taking me away.

My own alien-abduction-type experiences pale in comparison to those of Daniella's. To be perfectly honest, all the accounts I have read fall short of the intense things Daniella has been through. It will be for others to judge that for themselves, of course. Daniella is a lifelong experiencer of anomalous psychical phenomena (APP). She works as a professional psychic reader and is a capable spiritual medium as well as being certified in hypnotic regression. Daniella is a very skilled shamanic practitioner and developed many of her techniques during our five years spent living in the Ecuadorian Andes. She is also the only person I know who holds a license issued by the Peruvian government for the practice of traditional shamanic healing. From the crib until the present day, hers has been a most unusual life.

Psychic mediums and shamans regularly report receiving communications from beings identifying themselves as alien to this world. These contacts can be either extraterrestrial or interdimensional in nature. Contact with such entities is a frequent occurrence in the psychical community.

Daniella's earliest memories, from eighteen months old, include profoundly strange beings in the area just beyond her crib. She recalls many, many times when bizarre creatures were with her in the bedroom.

One of the beings encountered was a hairy apelike humanoid. It stood a little taller than three feet and had the disconcerting habit of bouncing around the room. It was no less frightening to observe it standing at the corner of the crib watching her. Daniella worried it might grab hold of her at any moment. She saw this same apelike entity dozens and dozens of times over several years. It has made me wonder if there is a connection to the tall, shaggy-haired entity in my childhood nightmares. Intriguingly, Terry Lovelace has described seeing monkeys in his bedroom during childhood abduction experiences, and he has also received reports of the same scenario from other alien abductees.

Other than the frightening ape, another visitor to Daniella's bedroom also left her trembling. This second ominous entity was a six-and-a-half foot tall, grayish-black humanoid with almond-shaped eyes that monitored her in bed.

Some will say that these nocturnal visits were just the vivid dreams of a child, fantasies rather than phantasms. My response to such dismissals would be to highlight the fact that for Daniella's entire life she has continued to see nonhuman entities and spirit people, many during the daylight hours. Her extraordinary psychic gifts have been validated time and again, as her clients gladly testify. Daniella readily states that the strangest of her experiences involves dozens of spontaneous shamanic journeys that occurred between early 2012 and the start of 2013. Though it is hard to put a complete name on these events, they seem to be a bizarre variation of the alien abduction experience. That is to say, the indication is that some external ETI controlled the process.

From the early part of 2012 until 2013, while we were living in Ecuador, Daniella went through a series of mind-bending and incredibly stressful extraterrestrial abduction-type experiences. These events did not involve aliens landing their saucers in the garden or them sucking her out of the bedroom window. That does not mean these events were any less tangible, and they were undoubtedly equally bizarre.

Daniella describes the events in her own words as follows. I observed her lapse into strange comatose states. During the abductions or shamanic journeys, Daniella would sometimes speak very quietly. From my investigations, I believe the language spoken is a form of ancient Mayan.

The very first of my strange journeys began after I had collapsed on my bed in absolute agony. Finally, I passed out from the pain, and I then experienced what felt like my entire body being shattered into tiny pieces. Whatever remained of me was dragged through some kind of energetic barrier. Perhaps it was my bedroom wall. The shocking transition from my physical life to this bizarre but equally real other-dimensional realm was beyond agonizing. It was a level and type of pain I will never forget. Quite honestly, at this point, I assumed I was probably dead.

I found myself in a circular-floored domed space. There was a strange teal color to the almost-imperceptible translucent walls of the structure. Now, in hindsight, I sometimes wonder if I could have been on a flying saucer craft. Beyond the limits of the intangible structure was what seemed to be empty space.

Present with me were several humanoid and quite human-like entities. These people were very tall and quite obviously not rational human beings. Most of the individuals were engaged in a discussion about various events unfolding on Earth and others they expected to occur in the future.

While my personality, or soul—that intangible part of myself—had been pulled from my mundane reality, my physical body remained behind with Bruce. This was the case for all the dozens of similar voyages that would follow over the months ahead. While I did sometimes have physical effects on my health and my body, I was never bodily taken to another location.

The second time these entities dragged my spirit away from my normal life, I found myself inhabiting someone else's body. The person I had taken control of was an extraordinarily tall and powerfully built young woman clothed in slightly risqué, Native American-type clothes. I was inside some sort of underground tunnel system.

Through a series of encounters, I was able to uncover that the woman I was inhabiting was a noble of the ancient Mayan culture. At a later stage in these journeys, I came to understand that the events were unfolding in the city of Palenque, Mexico, during the seventh century AD. This is a city made famous in ancient astronaut theories due to the belief that an alien ship is engraved into a sarcophagus lid within the central stepped pyramid.

The noblewoman I had merged with, Kat'Zil, was not a normal human. Her form was the result of alien modification of DNA. Indeed, most of the highest dignitaries in Palenque seemed to be of the same strange hybrid race as my personal "avatar."

These nobles were generally about six-and-a-half feet tall, essentially giants compared to the regular Maya citizens. Even today you can see the height difference accurately portrayed in Mayan artwork, with servants standing on large boxes to talk directly with their overlords. Good examples of such art can be seen on the walls of the Temple of the Foliated Cross.

Much of the official business of the city was conducted during meetings in a subterranean tunnel network. When I first published an account of my experiences in 2012, I mentioned tunnels with water flowing through them. Since then, several tunnels with water flowing through them have been confirmed by ground penetrating radar surveys conducted in 2016. The Mayan underworld was filled with stone calendars, strange artifacts, emerald green tablets, and other incredible wonders.

I spent just over a year of my time in Ecuador living two distinct lives, separated by several centuries. My two worlds were linked by a thread of shared high *strangeness and the fact that Bruce was present in both, even though he looked a bit different in his hybrid body, and his name there was Itz'Kal. I don't want to go too far into this matter, but this otherworldly "Bruce" was also different in that he had a volatile character and was annoyingly misogynistic.*

Living among the strange Maya-alien hybrids was not the only thing to contend with in Palenque. Inside a separate section of the underground network were experimental laboratories run by some very intimidating alien beings. The denizens of these subterranean chambers were very tall, bulbous-headed, gray-skinned humanoids.

I have since learned that these entities are known in modern ufology circles as tall grays. At that time I had no previous awareness of them. Working alongside these giant creatures were what appeared to be very approximate smaller versions of themselves. These servile entities are what is known as the short grays. It was unclear what hold the tall beings had over the shorter type; they were categorically not on an equal footing.

On several occasions, I noticed one other type of humanoid in this part of the tunnel system: human-like beings with scaly skin rather like that of lizards. My assumption is these were another variation of human hybrids engineered by one of the extraterrestrial species.

Throughout my journeys to Palenque, I was given a great deal of information, some of which could be considered extraterrestrial knowledge. One of the most important revelations that emerged was that the Maya leadership were associated with entities that had traveled to our world from the direction of the Pleiades star cluster. It was not clear which cosmic locations the gray beings were associated with, but it was somewhere different.

Now, whether this was me slipping back to a past life as it seemed or some type of astral time travel to the Palenque, I can't be sure. Perhaps my journeys involved some strange projection of that city beamed directly into my consciousness, like a bizarre, fully immersive virtual reality game.

Every explanation that I think of for what happened is equally strange, and even if I were to settle on one rather than another, it would still not explain the mechanics of the phenomenon. These were vividly real experiences that I lived through, and they have changed my life forever. Not necessarily in a particularly positive way.

I will never again be the person I was before these anomalous events unfolded. Most psychologically perturbing is the fact that I have children living in another reality. When I am there, I hold them in my arms and sing to them. Once I am back in my present life, I am separated from them by over a thousand years. Are they still there laughing and playing, or are they just dust? Imagine having to worry about members of your family that only exist in a separate dimension. Given a choice, I would definitely never have gone through any of this high strangeness.

The time travel–type experiences that Daniella went through have changed her as a person. Not only was her perception of reality shifted, but her personal health was considerably impacted. We have, of course, shared only the barest of details from these strange metaphysical journeys. To provide the full account would double the length of this book.

During the same period of Daniella's metaphysical journeys, many of which involved the tall grays trying to catch her and extract DNA samples, another very traumatic thing occurred: three months into a pregnancy, Daniella woke up feeling pain, and we rushed to a gynecological clinic. The doctor performed a scan and said the fetus must have spontaneously aborted, as there was nothing there. Daniella explained that it was impossible because she would have had to pass the remains. The doctor scanned again and then looked quite perturbed. She then asked if anything strange had happened.

The doctor explained that she could see a small circle where the fetus had been attached and that it looked almost as if it had been carefully plucked away. There were also odd features in the scan. When the scan was shown to Daniella, she could immediately see what looked incredibly like a bizarre face inside her womb. The fact that the doctor looked freaked out hardly helped to reassure her that this was a normal result. We were, of course, both left devasted by this situation, as any couple would be, but we also additionally had to wonder if our expected child was being raised by weird aliens on a ship somewhere.

There are huge overlaps among AAP, evidence of ETI, and psychic abilities that have not gone unnoticed by deep state scientific research projects. Metaphysical events are a significant subject within this field of investigation. Yet, if we were to judge the reality of APP solely on the bellwether of mainstream media coverage, it would seem there was almost total academic rejection.

The big question to be asked is whether the media is giving us an accurate picture of the current state of scientific understanding. Despite the common misconceptions to the contrary, there exists no consensus in science as to whether psychic abilities exist—no more so than there is a consensus about the existence of an all-powerful god running the universe.

It's no secret that the public is overwhelmingly accepting of the legitimacy of mystical and otherworldly phenomena. Most people identify as religious believers. Religious and spiritual events take us directly into the realms of psychical and spiritual affairs. Let's consider here an interesting Ipsos MORI survey of beliefs carried out in late 2018.

The Ipsos MORI poll, funded by the Scientific & Medical Network, involved three thousand science, engineering, medical, and technical research professionals. The survey sampled individuals based in France, Germany, and the United Kingdom. The results suggest that only about 25 percent of such professionals consider themselves to be atheists, and a further 16 percent were agnostic. This perhaps surprising finding means that more than half of the scientists had some type of religious or spiritual beliefs.[6]

It is probably a bit shocking for some people to realize that scientists are just as split over spiritual and metaphysical matters as the rest of the population. It does not mesh well with the perception generated by heavily biased and dogmatic "skeptical" media reporting.

Psychic abilities, intelligent aliens, and strange lights in the sky have consistently been made fun of by journalists for several decades. This incongruous presentation offered to the public has left many to feel they must be in the minority as believers of "the phenomena," while artificially empowering the loud-mouthed debunkers. The truth is, most of us either believe or know that psychic abilities exist. Just as so many people are aware, anomalous phenomena plague our skies. The intelligence community certainly understands all of this, as we will see.

CHAPTER 4

RETHINKING THE ANOMALOUS

When the evidence for an anomaly becomes
overwhelming, and the anomaly cannot be easily
accommodated by the existing scientific worldview, this
is a very important sign that either our assumptions
about reality are wrong or our assumptions about how
we come to understand things are wrong.

—DEAN RADIN, PhD

While the Advanced Aviation Threat Identification Program (AATIP) may have focused on research relating to AAP and theorizing on technology that might explain the observed astonishing capabilities, other secretive projects have concentrated more on APP. Several of the scientists linked to AATIP and To the Stars Academy of Arts and Science (TTSA) have also previously been involved in mind-bending psychical research projects. Two of the scientists I would like to single out here are Dr. Kit Green and Harold (Hal) Puthoff, PhD.

While reading what follows, please keep in mind some of the strange phenomena already discussed in connection with reported alien abductions and interaction with AAP.

These subjects are all intimately connected—hence the multidisciplinary interest shown by the military-contracted scientific researchers.

Project Stargate was the code name attributed to an above-top-secret military program that began in 1978. The Defense Intelligence Agency (DIA) and SRI International, a California contractor, initiated an investigation into the potential for psychic phenomena to benefit military and domestic intelligence endeavors. Project Stargate, once a deep black project but now made public, involved the recruitment of a team of psychical test subjects. Participants were taken from the top tier of intuitive people, the best of the best when it came to the demonstration of supernormal abilities. The focus was on researching the active use of psychic abilities for the battle theater. The scientists involved quickly realized that certain individuals had the intuitive ability to remotely view distant locations with astonishing accuracy.

Significant investigative journalistic efforts have been made to better understand this highly unusual military-sponsored program. These investigations have resulted in two top-rated books: *The Men Who Stare at Goats,* by Jon Ronson, and *Phenomena: The Secret History of the U.S. Government's Investigations into Extrasensory Perception and Psychokinesis,* by Annie Jacobsen. At the time of this writing, a new documentary, *Third Eye Spies,* has just been released that centers on one of the senior research scientists that ran Project Stargate, Russell Targ. Together, these books and films provide a startling window into one of the most highly classified and paradigm-shattering scientific investigations of all time.

Jon Ronson took his peculiar book title from one of the experiments involving the "psychic soldiers." The individuals were tasked with stopping a goat's heart by merely willing it to happen. Special Forces Sergeant Glenn Wheaton, a remote viewer with the program, claims to have personally witnessed one of their martial arts trainers, Mike Echanis, dispatch a goat by focused intention alone.[1]

The remote viewers were successful in correctly identifying the locations for secret military installations, including details of a prototype Russian submarine, and even reading top-secret files kept in secure underground facilities. One of the most stunning success stories would ultimately be a factor in the closure of the project.

During a 1995 conversation with US media, former US president Jimmy Carter revealed that in the late 1970s a remote viewer from the military had correctly pinpointed the map coordinates of a crashed Russian TU-22 bomber. The operative involved was an Air Force–enlisted woman named Rosemary Smith. "The woman went into a trance and gave some latitude and longitude figures," explained Carter. "We focused our satellite cameras on that point, and the plane was there."[2]

President Carter had inadvertently outed an active above-top-secret military program to the general public. With the attention of the media now squarely on this strange story, it was not long before Project Stargate would be officially closed, despite more than two decades of support from senior military and sitting presidents. Evidently, it was decided that though the intel generated had been essential to various successful operations, the public was not ready to be told the government knew psychic abilities were a real thing.

Perhaps most famous from the small SRI team are Ingo Swann, a legendary remote viewer, and Uri Geller, renowned for his psychokinetic abilities, including bending metal with his thoughts. A science journalist friend of mine interviewed Geller some years ago and witnessed him bend a fork placed on the table, without physically touching it at all.

Declassified documents reveal that at one stage there was considerable fear that people with gifts like Geller's might interfere with the sensitive control mechanisms of intercontinental ballistic missiles (ICBMs).[3] This is especially intriguing when we think of the strange effects AAP can seemingly wield over nuclear missile silos.

Ingo Swann went on to write books about his remote viewing work, and in his book *Penetration: The Question of Extraterrestrial and Human Telepathy*, he recounts a clandestine $1,000-per-day contract to remote view coordinates on the dark side of the moon.

Swann's client, code name Axelrod, first asked if he knew a man named George Leonard. Swann did not and had no idea why this mattered. He was eventually taken, blindfolded, to a secret underground facility from which he would be attempting to view ten sets of lunar coordinates. Understandably, Swann expected to see very little other than dust, rocks, and craters, but he suspected perhaps a secret satellite had crashed or that the government wanted to select a good site for a lunar base.

Once the remote viewing began, things took a turn for the decidedly bizarre. Swann encountered what appeared to be tire tracks and then a strange, smooth obsidian-like wall. A second location included a greenish glowing mist beneath rows of green lights on some type of tall towers. Swann stopped and apologized, assuming he must have somehow returned to Earth. Axelrod looked distinctly distressed. Swann finally began to realize that this was what he had been hired to observe and assumed it must be a Russian base.

The most mind-bending observation was a tower about forty floors tall rising up from a crater, not far from the glowing dust clouds and vehicle tracks. Axelrod mumbled to himself, "You can see that, then?"[4]

Swann struggled to process how nations that could barely get men into space would have constructed huge structures on the lunar surface. Finally, his mental fog cleared, and he realized that the site could not be the doing of human beings. Swann guessed that Axelrod must have been an agent with a government task force assigned to the clandestine investigation of extraterrestrial matters. Some months later a researcher named George Leonard published a study of NASA images that reveal alien technology on the lunar surface: *Somebody Else Is on the Moon*.

Unlike Daniella, I am no expert in remote viewing, but in 2010 I was fortunate enough to participate in a remote viewing workshop headed by Russell Targ. Most of the participants picked up accurate information about the hidden target (kept in a closed box), and one member of our group managed to accurately draw the item: a metal statue of a Hindu goddess holding a sun wheel. It was ironic that he was an engineer attending the event with his wife, herself a professional psychic.

Russell Targ's former colleague Dean Radin, PhD, has since become the senior research scientist at the Institute of Noetic Sciences (IONS). This organization, dedicated to investigating extrasensory perception, was set up by NASA astronaut Edgar Mitchell. Mitchell became convinced of the reality of psychic abilities after a powerful psychical experience of oneness with all things while traveling in space. Mitchell was also an ardent believer in intelligent extraterrestrials visiting Earth, as can be readily seen in this comment made to the *Guardian* newspaper: "We are being visited, it is now time to put away this embargo of truth about the alien presence. I call upon our government to open up . . . and become a part of this planetary community that is now trying to take our proper role as a spacefaring civilisation."[5]

IONS carries out astonishing investigations into mysterious states of consciousness and psychical abilities. Radin says of these intuitive skills, "What we're talking about is something like a talent, similar to musical talent or sports talent. So, there will be some people who are at the Olympic level; most of us aren't there."[6]

Returning to Annie Jacobsen's investigation of Project Stargate, we learn that, though it ended in 1995, the US military retains an interest in heightened intuitive capabilities. This fact was reported on in detail in Jacobsen's April 2017 article for *Time* magazine, in which we learn that the Office of Naval Research (ONR) invested $3.85 million into a four-year research program exploring premonition with suspected battlefield applications.[7]

Unlike the SRI researchers, the naval scientists at the ONR's Expeditionary Maneuver Warfare and Combating Terrorism Department were not theorizing how psychic abilities might function. Dr. Peter Squire, a program officer with the department, clarifies that "we have to understand what gives rise to this so-called sixth sense."[8] In other words, they just want their soldiers to acquire these skills.

The ONR has good reason to accept the factual nature of intuition in engagement situations: they would have the benefit of not only conclusions from earlier research programs such as SRI's but also their own field reports. The researchers explain that their project emerged from the astonishing number of personnel claiming they or comrades had been saved from certain death by sudden intuitive flashes of insight. Events recorded would include the sensing of hidden roadside bombs, sniper positions, and impending ambushes. Squire explains that the Pentagon's focus is to maximize the power of the sixth sense for operational use and spread this ability throughout military units. "Are there ways to improve premonition through training?" asks Lieutenant Commander Brent Olde of ONR's Warfighter Performance Department for Human and Bioengineered Systems.[9]

The Department of Defense is doing all it can to bring the development of precognitive skills to active-duty marines. The terminology the Navy uses for this skill set is *advanced perceptual competences* or *sensemaking*. New terminology is deliberately used to provide a degree of separation from historically derided terms like extrasensory perception (ESP) and psychokinesis (PK).

For soldiers in active war zones, there is no time to ponder and debate the mechanisms of human consciousness that might allow for psychic knowing. If a fellow soldier regularly senses actual dangers that prevent their and your death, their skills are tangible enough. People inevitably follow "the lucky one" when excrement begins to meet the fan; nobody much cares how they work their mojo.

It should come as no surprise to learn that Russia also ran a secretive psychic spy and super-soldier program. In early 2019, the government-sanctioned magazine *Soldiers of Russia* revealed that Soviet scientists were active in similar projects from the 1960s to the 1980s. What the Soviets had termed "combat parapsychology" allegedly went beyond even remote viewing to successfully practicing telepathic communication with dolphins.[10]

Interestingly, the CIA and DOD have concluded from their investigations that intuitive abilities are often weak, sometimes intense, and in a small number of people, utterly extraordinary. I am fortunate to know several extremely gifted psychics, some of whom have demonstrated Olympic-level skills. I have gained access to important research material that came to me thanks to the unique abilities that my friends and contacts exhibit.

We will return to matters of psychic ability later, but first we need to look again at the complex and shifting attitudes toward the subject of alien contact.

CHAPTER 5

THE FIRST CONTACT
CONTINUUM

*There is abundant evidence that we are
being contacted, that civilizations have
been visiting us for a very long time.*

—BRIAN O'LEARY, former NASA astronaut
and Princeton physics professor

Humans have long looked up at the heavens and wondered whether any beings might live among the stars.
Most ancient cultures have passed down stories of gods and
spirits that populate the inky blackness of the night sky or
reside on far-off worlds.

The earliest spiritual traditions, commonly bundled
together under the term *shamanism,* included the understanding that humans could contact entities inhabiting
sky worlds. It was widely accepted that psychical voyagers
could bring back useful information from these metaphysical interactions. If the contact claims offered by shamanic
cultures are based on facts—as many of us believe—then
the first contact between modern humans and extraterrestrial entities likely happened many millennia ago.

It is possible some of the first exchanges between humans and extraterrestrials were initiated by a shaman entering an altered state of consciousness and traveling to a neighboring dimension. Having had many such encounters with non-human entities during my own shamanic practices, I have no reason to doubt the validity of the experiences of other ancestral healers and mystics. It is crucial to point out here that not all aliens need be physical beings; some could reside outside of the constraints of our physical universe, existing as discarnate intelligence.

In our modern world, most people tend to imagine the first contact between our species and advanced alien races involving nuts-and-bolts-type scenarios. Perhaps the most common depiction is that of the interstellar vehicle landing on the White House lawn, followed by a humanoid entity emerging to shake hands with the president of the United States. Incredibly unlikely as it is, a great many people expect the first contact to be much the same as how we greet other people living on our planet.

We humans usually physically go to where the other person is whom we want to meet, generally in some type of transportation device. Upon arrival, we announce ourselves and then have a face-to-face physical interaction with them. The reality is that any assumption that aliens behave much like us is just a projection of human thinking. We should be wary of expecting behavior that seems reasonable from another source of intelligence that would likely have no experience of human cultural norms. Though it is possible an ETI might quietly observe us and then use this knowledge to represent itself as similar to us, most scientists and psychologists working on the question of ETI contact scenarios tend to see human-like behavior as most unlikely.

One very popular expectation is that first contact will involve one of our advanced listening stations. It could be perhaps that a radio-telescope picks up a signal from deep space being emitted by another technological species. The message received might be a deliberate greeting sent to us, or it could be an intercepted communication intended for other members of the originating species.

As we have discussed, various SETI projects currently monitor the cosmos for any errant signals that show signs of order or intentional structure. There have already been a few tantalizing detections, but unfortunately, unless a message repeats, it is not possible to designate it as artificial in nature. There are some tentative hopes among scientists that the recently identified phenomena of fast radio bursts (FRBs) might be linked to a form of intelligence. To date, we still do not have convincing evidence of repeating transmissions that exhibit structure.[1]

Have you ever wondered what an extraterrestrial first contact event might smell like? This may seem like an obtuse question, but though there is always a great deal of speculation about how visitors from space would physically present themselves, we really should be thinking more outside the box. It is probable you have never given much thought to what role smell might play in a first contact situation. It seems like out-of-context thinking perhaps, yet this is entirely why such a question should be asked. Extraterrestrial beings would likely behave in ways contrary to our expectations and even beyond our comprehension. Indeed, their behavior would be entirely "alien."

If we make the mistake of expecting an extraterrestrial to behave just like a human and to use greeting methods identical to ours, we could easily mistake contact for something else. In fact, our naïve expectations could ensure we miss an attempted greeting entirely.

We know that, even among animals on this planet, many use smell or displays of color to greet fellow members of their species. Some animals produce sounds that are inaudible to humans, and others emit invisible pheromones as their standard method of welcoming members of their species. To be ready for communication from alien beings, we must think entirely outside the box. I implore you to open your mind to an unlimited range of potential contact scenarios. Perhaps the one constant in any hypothetical model for such an event should be the expectation for some degree of high strangeness.

Fortunately, there are several useful depictions of extraterrestrial contact scenarios available from within modern popular culture. I highlight here several Hollywood films for your consideration, each of which had considerable input from scientists and prominent philosophical thinkers, alongside a healthy dose of creative genius. The plots in these movies ask audiences to forget about the "landing on the White House lawn" scenario. Instead, there is a push to consider much more alien thinking. Each of these stories includes a degree of overlap with the real-life extraterrestrial contact discussed in this book, and I suspect that some of the material contained in certain films has been seeded by people "in the know." Some of the overlaps with data I have uncovered are just so close that it's a struggle to accept them as entirely coincidental.

Close Encounters of the Third Kind (1977)

In this Steven Spielberg classic, we are presented with a multilevel contact scenario involving a wide range of strange phenomena. The initial events of the film include the sudden reappearance of several planes and boats long vanished inside the infamous Bermuda Triangle.

The circumstances surrounding the reappeared craft are investigated by a team of scientists and ufologists. This team of experts is led to an encounter with a group of spiritual adepts in India. The Indian monks chant a series of weird musical sounds, which they claim to have heard coming down from the sky. The same sequence of tones is later broadcast into space by a research team in the United States. The interstellar message prompts a reply from an unknown intelligence, incorporating a set of coordinates for a location in Wyoming.

Meanwhile, in Muncie, Indiana, there is a visitation involving strange aerial craft emitting flashing colored lights. These anomalous aerial objects cause much chaos, including disruption of the power grid. While working on the resultant electrical problems, Roy Neary, a local electrician, has a close encounter with a craft.

The interaction between Roy and the object provokes an obsessed state in him. It seems that some psychic transmission—a download—has been embedded in Roy's mind. Later, Roy goes on to construct a model of a mountain that he keeps seeing in his mind's eye. The model strangely matches an image of Devil's Mountain, Wyoming, shown on his television. Roy feels compelled to reach the off-limits landing site on Devil's Mountain. While en route he discovers that many other alien contactees have also received the message and are trying to access the now closed-off location.

The film climaxes with the alien mothership arriving and exchanging a series of sounds and light pulses with government personnel on the ground. The vessel lands and the door opens, allowing a stream of abductees to emerge.

Roy is then cleared to join a group of scientists that have decided to depart with the extraterrestrial visitors to learn more about them.

Though perhaps somewhat dated as a film, *Close Encounters of the Third Kind* gives a good sense of the type of phenomenon we might expect to accompany a greeting from beyond the stars. We are given a show of power by the beings, an unequivocal demonstration of their superior technologies. The ETI provides a method for responding to them and beginning communication. The visitors show no interest in meeting a singular leader.

While the extraterrestrials do communicate with the local power structures (mainly government scientists), they also send psychic invitations to a broad segment of the public. In a final overt show of their benevolent intentions, the aliens return everyone they have ever abducted for study.

Finally, there is an offer of a conditional working relationship between the respective species. All the phenomena in the film, though replete with high strangeness, start to make sense once put together into the context of advanced aliens making their first contact.

Contact (1997)

This movie is based on a book of the same name by famous astrophysicist Carl Sagan. The story centers on Dr. Ellie Arroway, a scientist involved with SETI who finds a repeating radio signal. The source of the emission is in the direction of the star Vega, situated in the constellation of Lyra.

The intercepted message contains a hidden schematic for an enormous machine. The device is eventually constructed by the allied governments of the world, working in harmony. The mechanism appears to be designed to allow one occupant to enter inside and presumably contact those sending the messages. In an unexpected turn of events, a religious fanatic carries out a suicide bomb attack on the installation, destroying it and killing the chosen representative. Fortunately, the destruction of the mysterious machine is not the end of the story, as a reclusive billionaire has privately funded a copy of the machine. This secret project eventually allows Ellie to operate the device, which, as it transpires, can move her through space and time.

After Ellie passes through a series of wormholes, a meeting takes place between Ellie and a non-physical extraterrestrial being presenting itself in the form of her deceased father. The climax of the film takes place on a beach that is being projected to Ellie based on memories extracted from her own mind.

The alien being provides little more than confirmation that there are many advanced races in the universe, explaining that they contact progressive species whenever it seems appropriate. It is clarified that humanity is not considered enlightened enough to gain immediate admission into their galaxy-wide network. The being explains that Earth will be monitored until such time as another step can be taken toward friendship.

We can recognize in *Contact* several essential themes. First, we are introduced to the potential religious implications of and reactions to the discovery of life beyond our planet. There is then an exploration of the idea that secret projects involving advanced alien technologies are being run by shady billionaires. These types of secret scientific projects are something many people suspect is really happening today.

The mode of transport the beings use is based on wormholes. Wormholes are a theoretical method of moving vast distances quickly and can potentially even move an object through time.

The ETI takes a cautious position and wants to take gradual steps. The aliens then initiate monitoring of our planet while they take time to consider full open contact between species.

Interstellar (2014) and Arrival (2016)

These two much more recent films are also important to consider. Both involve the manipulation of time by highly advanced technologies. There are puzzles to be solved that require humanity to find the very best in themselves. Not only do we see some novel ideas presented but also advances in modern scientific understanding are reflected in the plots.

In *Interstellar*, the beings involved are eventually deduced to be descendants of modern humans now existing in a fifth dimension. These distant relatives have reached back through time to help their ancestors (creating several temporal paradoxes in the process).

The extraterrestrial beings in *Arrival* are also deeply involved in the manipulation of time. These octopus-like entities have seen a future time line upon which descendants of modern humans will do something that saves the alien species.

Initially, the creatures position several of their craft around the planet and then distribute clues to the various governments, which requires global collaboration and unification of intentions. This prevents the possibly catastrophic opening of dialogue with any sole national power.

Both *Arrival* and *Interstellar* suggest that genuinely advanced civilizations will have some degree of control over the fabric of reality and time itself. These films also suggest that contact with an incredibly sophisticated technological culture is likely to revolve around their self-interests.

— — —

We should carefully consider the motivations of any species that reaches out across the cosmos to shake our hands. It is possible the motives for cosmic contact would be benevolent, or they could involve more negative intentions. We might, of course, find it hard to do anything about evil plans formulated by a much more advanced galactic civilization.

Many of the concepts and specific details presented in these four Hollywood movies also feature in the real-life contact event at the heart of this book. The intelligence involved here in our world undoubtedly has a level of self-interest. There is strong evidence that the alien presence controls technologies that allow movement through time and space. It is indeed my opinion that some of the strange objects in our skies are technologies operated by this cosmic intelligence. Anomalous aerial vehicles may be a visual demonstration of the power wielded by off-world or inter-dimensional forces. I see strong evidence for more than one player at the table and that the interests seem entirely divergent. Where you find devils, don't be surprised to also discover angels.

It is possible that some representatives of these nonhuman entities are already in contact with government agencies, unknown to us. There is suggestive evidence of such a conspiracy, but there is most certainly contact underway involving members of the general public. This communication is occurring through psychical mechanisms.

It is my strongest suspicion that once we as a global species recognize and acknowledge the invitation to communicate, a more straightforward and overt relationship will be established.

I can't leave this examination of alien contact–themed films without discussing the most important of all, *2001: A Space Odyssey* (1968). The first thing that should be said about this film is that the scriptwriters, Stanley Kubrick and Arthur C. Clarke, both had incredibly well-positioned friends in elite circles. It is no great stretch to imagine that they might have been fed information from secret projects involving extraterrestrial beings.

The script for this film contains a narrative that overlaps considerably with the non-fiction information uncovered in my investigation. Don't be surprised if you find me mentioning this movie several more times before we reach the final conclusion. Kubrick and Clarke seem to have known something that the rest of us have not been privy to, at least not until now.

2001: A Space Odyssey starts with the revelation that an advanced extraterrestrial intelligence left a technological object on Earth in prehistoric times. The alien machine is in the form of a giant black, rectangular glass-like monolith. In the initial scenes of the movie, ancient hominins encounter the monolith during a cosmic convergence. Proximity to the monolith—touching its surface—somehow modifies human consciousness and rapidly changes the behavior of the hominins. The group affected by the alien technology spontaneously starts using animal bones as clubs. Their intelligence has been upgraded, and they are now ready for tool use. The wielding of the first weapons signifies the initiation of a path toward human technological superiority of the planet.

One of the bone clubs is thrown into the air, and as we watch it rise the scene cuts away, and the club is replaced in the frame by an advanced orbital weapons platform. We have evolved, but have we traveled down the right path? Would we have been somehow better off without the interference? Later in the screenplay, a second monolith is encountered hidden on the moon. Astronauts touching this new monolith cause a signal to be emitted toward Jupiter. We are left to assume the monolith is passing on the message that humanity has moved out into space. Humanity's overseers can begin the next stage of their cryptic project.

It is our educated opinion that *2001: A Space Odyssey* skirts incredibly close to the truth, from the nature of the monoliths to the themes of AI and genetic engineering of early hominins. This is something that will be further discussed later.

Having tentatively explored several hypothetical alien contact scenarios, we would like to lay our cards on the table, so to speak. In the previous chapters, we have explored plentiful evidence of a first contact event well underway. Most of that evidence is anecdotal; some of it is tangible. In the chapters that follow, we share a wealth of astonishing objective scientific data with you. Once you know all that we do, we can then make a case for humanity initiating full engagement with the various benevolent extraterrestrial, interdimensional, and extratemporal parties. We should also firmly dismiss the overtures of the entirely self-interested parties also present.

You will gain access to substantial evidence of contact that occurred between an extraterrestrial intelligence and our early hominin ancestors many hundreds of thousands of years ago. The communication has long since begun, and it is ongoing.

We contend that much of the interaction between the aliens and human beings occurs in parallel realities and psychical worlds. It is possible for participants to enter these "workspaces" utilizing altered states of consciousness. A meeting can be initiated by either party. You might wonder if these meetings happen in waking reality or during dreams. The answer is both, and neither: it is a kind of crack between worlds. For the intelligence there is hardly a difference between waking and dreaming. There is only processing of perceptions and the shifting of awareness.

Extraterrestrial contact is not an isolated event. It is a continuum, and we are a long way into this process already. We are about to reach a critical step on this path. We need to move to widespread human acceptance of the existence of the intelligent visitors. For some this requires objective evidence. Others will just "get it."

If this disclosure happens the right way, it will give the green light to benevolent cosmic cultures to fully reveal themselves—to display their true nature, which in many cases transcends the popular concepts of physical-biological beings arriving in metal ships.

We may well be at the beginning of the real space age in which humanity begins open, overt relationships with our cosmic neighbors. We just need to choose the path with a heart.

SECTION TWO

MESSAGE RECEIVED

We could explore space, together,
both inner and outer, forever, in peace.

—BILL HICKS

CHAPTER 6

ENCOUNTERS WITH ALIEN TECHNOLOGIES

The most sophisticated civilizations will be post-biological, forms of artificial intelligence (AI). Further, alien civilizations will tend to be forms of superintelligence: intelligence that is able to exceed the best human-level intelligence in every field—social skills, general wisdom, scientific creativity, and so on.

—SUSAN SCHNEIDER, professor of
philosophy and cognitive science

Scientists routinely use technology to replace the human exploration of space. Not only do we use orbital telescopes to extend our view of the cosmos but we send out robotic probes far more often than human beings. Though no man or woman has yet walked the surface of Mars (to the best of my knowledge), mechanical rovers and landers have already begun the investigation of that world on our behalf.

It is becoming evident that the future of space exploration will likely have very little to do with human beings flying around in rocket ships. Stephen Hawking spoke extensively on precisely this matter. As discussed in his final book, *Brief Answers to the Big Questions,* Hawking's view was that alien beings would likely send out self-replicating intelligent machines to explore the cosmos. These machines would represent a new form of life based on mechanical and electrical components, rather than macromolecules and DNA.

Seth Shostak, senior astronomer at the SETI Institute, has previously voiced his opinion that any detectable biological intelligence likely has a very short duration. The creations of organic life—machine intelligence—would be far more durable and long lasting. It is his view that intelligent machines will likely come to dominate the universe. Former NASA chief historian Steven J. Dick agrees with Shostak and predictively estimates that perhaps only one in a million civilizations across the universe will be biological. This calculation emerges from the simple fact that biological intelligence is likely limited to a brief existence.[1]

With this realization comes the logical implication that we are far more likely to be visited from space by unmanned probes, or some type of advanced artificial intelligence, than we are to see biological organisms arriving and giving our chosen representatives a high five (assuming the aliens have hands).

The black monoliths of Arthur C. Clarke's *2001: A Space Odyssey* were not simply machines left by an alien biological intelligence but the technologically evolved, post-biological remnants of an intelligent biological species. The long-forgotten first explorers of Earth had transitioned to a post-biological existence, as Clarke explains: "First their brains, and then their thoughts alone, they transferred into shining new homes of metal and of plastic."[2]

James Benford, PhD, is a plasma physicist interested in investigating the possibility that there might be long-duration extraterrestrial devices, known as *Bracewell probes*, left somewhere in our solar system. Ronald Bracewell was a professor of electrical engineering at the Space, Telecommunications, and Radioscience Laboratory at Stanford University. Bracewell hypothesized that any technologically advanced extraterrestrial civilization would likely have its own SETI program. He felt that any such initiatives would likely involve artificially intelligent probes being dispatched to potentially life-supporting candidate planetary systems.

These Bracewell probes, if combined with sufficient self-repair functions, might remain in place for eons, rather like cosmic sentinels. If a civilization eventually arose on any target planet and then reached technological levels, the probe would beam back a confirmation to its builders. It might also even be programmed to initiate direct contact. Benford is intrigued by the possibility of discovering any such artifacts in our own solar system because they would allow for real-time communication with extraterrestrial intelligence. Scientists might be limited to interacting with the onboard AI, but perhaps they could use the probe's relay system to send messages back to its creators.[3]

While there have been a small number of claims that relate to potential extraterrestrial technologies here on Earth, we share Benford's interest in those that can share higher knowledge. At least two such objects have already been recovered and accessed. Before delving into that matter, though, let's quickly explore some other tantalizing technosignatures.

We previously touched on possible alien implants, and these would certainly count as physical examples of alien technology. There are also a growing number of physical samples claimed to be fragments from the mysterious UAVs. We will explore some craft debris evidence in detail.

At a recent conference, representatives from TTSA announced that one of the metal samples they have been investigating is exceptionally anomalous: a small sample of strange magnesium-zinc-bismuth alloy with a layering of just one to ten microns. There is no precedent for such an alloy existing, and the production process required is not understood.[4]

Analysis to date suggests the material acts as a waveguide for terahertz frequencies and can change its effective mass upon being irradiated. The material is posited to have antigravity capabilities. My sources assure me that several major aerospace companies are currently involved with the examination of this material. The indication so far is that the manufacturing of this material is beyond known human capabilities.

Though some fragments of alien technology may end up in the hands of scientists as the result of destroyed aerial vehicles, it is also a reason to suspect that extraterrestrials might deliberately plant their technologies here on Earth. The most obvious purposes would be for surveillance or to somehow influence the development of terrestrial life. This was the direction taken for the human interactions with the monoliths in *2001: A Space Odyssey.*

These "sentinel technologies" might be so baffling in appearance, or so well camouflaged, that people would typically fail to recognize them as technology. A fascinating account exists of an encounter had with what I suspect to be just such an artifact. In the book *The Crystal and the Way of Light: Sutra, Tantra, and Dzogchen,* Chögyal Namkhai Norbu, a Tibetan Dzogchen master, recounts the discovery.

Norbu's uncle, a great Buddhist master named Khyentse Chökyi Wangchug, was known to be a *terton.* Essentially, a terton is a highly intuitive meditation master able to locate ancient hidden texts and objects (*terma*). Wangchug had a vision that revealed the location of an important terma and asked his nephew whether he should announce the news or just quietly retrieve it alone. Norbu suggested that a public recovery would lead to the development of greater Buddhist faith among the local people. This path was agreed upon, and eventually a crowd of people departed to the target location. Upon sensing they had reached the right area, Wangchug indicated a point high on the side of a mountain. With some help from the crowd he was able to get close. The spot seemed to be just a smooth rock face. Wangchug borrowed a small climber's ice pick and threw it up at the place. It lodged into what had looked like a solid rock. A young man was sent up to carefully investigate the spot, and as he pulled the pick away, the "stone" of the wall crumbled away to powder.

Wangchug advised the young man not to touch the terma directly. Instead he used the pick to pull it out and then let it drop into a sheet spread out below. Into the sheet fell a smooth, round, white object. The terma was a luminous white orb, made of no material known to those present and approximately the size of a large grapefruit. It is virtually impossible not to think of this artifact as being reminiscent of World War II Foo Fighters and the spherical drones that were seen leaving UAVs, though in a more or less dormant state.

The orb was taken back to the village, and Wangchug placed it into a securely locked wooden container, which he then sealed with wax. Wangchug believed the object would reveal its purpose when the time was right. Several months later, they opened the box to find the sphere had mysteriously vanished.

Wangchug took the strange dematerialization in stride, being a man widely accredited with supernormal abilities. His opinion was that the Dakinis had recovered the artifact, as it was not the right moment for its revelation. The term *Dakini* can be approximately rendered into English as "sky dancer" or "she who flies in the limitless realms of space."[5] Might these Dakinis that retrieved the orb relate to AAP or act as representatives of alien intelligence?

The Tibetan luminous sphere may not have been ready to reveal its secrets, but we are fortunate that a different artifact has been more forthcoming. Now we come to the most critical alien object ever identified on this planet by a long shot. The object in question should be thought of as an astonishing example of a Bracewell probe. We do not know exactly what parameters had to be met for it to initiate contact, but clearly it was triggered by something.

In 1994, a mysterious visitor arrived at the home of Valerie Barrow (in Canyonleigh, New South Wales, in Australia), a psychic medium and holistic therapist. The visitor was a media professional named Helen, and she brought with her an object about the size of a shoebox. Whatever it was had been wrapped in paperbark and further covered by a white calico cloth tied with string.

The woman claimed that the object was a sacred Aboriginal churinga stone that she was trying to return to its traditional Aboriginal keepers, believed to reside somewhere in the region around Uluru (Ayers Rock), close to Alice Springs in the Northern Territory.

At the time Valerie was living in a house she had named *Alcheringa*, an Australian Aboriginal word from the Central and Northern Territories regions. Alcheringa refers to the period in which the first ancestors of humanity were created by powerful cosmic spirits, also more widely known as the *Dreamtime*. The word Alcheringa is closely related to the term *churinga*,[6] which denotes a sacred artifact imbued with valuable information.

Churingas come in different forms with distinct importance and purported functions. Some are fixed in place and represent the inhabitance of the dreaming being associated with a site and totemic spirits of a local population. The Aranda people refer to these *knanja*-type churinga in terms somewhat akin to the American Indian totem pole (which are also sometimes used by Aboriginal people).

There are links between these knanja and fertility rites as well as reincarnation lore. The souls of local people are sometimes considered to be fractals of the consciousness housed in the churinga. I can't help but see the mental image of the early hominins gathered around Kubrick's black sentinels as I think about this type of monolithic churinga. Smaller, more portable churinga of wood or stone *indulla-rrakura* are said to carry the individual spirits of nonhuman dreamtime entities. Typically, these objects are decorated with sacred red ochre symbols such as boomerangs, concentric circles, and wavy lines. This is the type we are more concerned with.

The Aboriginal people understand that the genuinely ancient churinga are considered the most sacred. These original churinga carry privileged information reserved only for certain qualified elders with the correct levels of spiritual initiation. These spiritual elders are known as "clever men/women" and are akin to the shamans or medicine men of other cultures.

The oldest of all these stone artifacts are claimed to be imbued with the consciousness of ancestral spirits from the Alcheringa creation times, the time before time. These Alcheringa beings can purportedly take incarnations into a human form while still having some part of themselves remaining rooted in the matrix of their stone receptacle.

Though today many churinga stones are acknowledged to be copies of the legendary original examples, it will soon become evident that the one that reached Valerie was no modern replica. The Aboriginal lore we have explored should be considered more closely for a moment. It sounds very much like a metaphysical, cultural narrative woven around extraterrestrial artifacts. Consider for a moment that perhaps the Aboriginal people had come to possess a compact silica-based Bracewell probe, complete with an onboard AI. At some stage, the resident consciousness of the ancient churinga stone acquired its preprogrammed signal to activate and began communicating with the local people.

It might also be that there are incredibly ancient beings that long ago transcended biology and can direct their consciousness into any physical matter they wish to occupy. This is my favored position and the one that best fits the Aboriginal lore. These scenarios both match well with the belief that the object is a receptacle of an ancient spirit from the creation times and that it carried incredible secret knowledge. Either way, we have the expected signature of highly advanced extraterrestrial or interdimensional intelligence.

Upon meeting, Helen explained to Valerie that a chain of synchronicity had brought her to the house with its unusual name. Helen felt that Valerie was the right person to temporarily look after the sacred object until she recovered from a severe health condition. Valerie later discovered that it was also hoped that if Helen did not improve, then the responsibility of custodianship would be transferred.

Valerie took pity on Helen and agreed to keep the artifact in her home until it was again retrieved. At that time, she had no idea it was anything more than an old stone wrapped in paperbark. She respectfully placed it into a small box and put it away in her healing room for safekeeping. Valerie never directly touched, or even looked at, this artifact, and it always remained within the wrappings. This felt to her the culturally sensitive thing to do, as such artifacts are reserved for Aboriginal ceremonial purposes. Even among Aboriginal people, only those appointed would ever handle these artifacts. Indeed, most indigenous people are scared of being near such powerful objects.

Interestingly, remember that Khyentse Chökyi Wangchug instructed people not to touch the strange glowing sphere he had helped to recover. It may be that alien-engineered objects involve energy that is in some way harmful when directly handled.

There is some reason to suspect a mutagenic effect of alien energy sources, with resultant modification of human DNA. This possibility has been discussed in ongoing cutting-edge research being carried out by Dr. Christopher "Kit" Green (formerly the CIA's branch chief for life science in the Office of Scientific Intelligence) and his collaborator Garry Nolan, PhD, a geneticist at Stanford University. Nolan is famous for analyzing the controversial Atacama "alien" mummy.

Nolan and Green have both worked in advisory capacities for TTSA. Green is formerly a team member of Project Stargate. They have identified a possibility that people encountering anomalous phenomena have resultant DNA anomalies. One suspicion emerging from their research is the possibility of an epigenetic effect resulting from contact with extraterrestrial energies.[7] (So remember, kids, don't touch the monolith!)

In 2012, Daniella and I coauthored the book *2012 Rising: The Last Tzolkin: Warnings from the Maya & The Pleiadians.* Included in the book were details of our personal contact with extraterrestrial intelligence. One of our readers recognized a connection between some of our accounts and the work of the Australian father-and-son research team Steven and Evan Strong. Communication was established, and after some conversations, we all decided to work on a book together. This collaborative relationship resulted in our coauthoring the 2013 book *Ancient Aliens in Australia: Pleiadian Origins of Humanity.*

During the latter part of the writing process, one of our coauthors mentioned a book called *ALCHERINGA... When the First Ancestors Were Created* (2002). They revealed that it was the overlap between my personal experiences and the content of that book that had convinced them we were telling the truth. We bought a copy of the Alcheringa book from its author, Valerie Barrow, and read the entire book in a single enthralled sitting.

Through this chain of events, we eventually ended up involved with the research project detailed in the current book. No matter how odd the individual events involved, there is a more coherent bigger picture visible once we zoom out and see these events in greater perspective. Even the shamanic journeys to Palenque and many of my personal experiences are yet other facets of this extraterrestrial contact continuum.

You can probably get some idea of what *ALCHERINGA... When the First Ancestors Were Created* is about just from its title. At the core of the story is claimed extraterrestrial involvement in the origins of *Homo sapiens.* We were both amazed to discover that this book involved some of the same types of entities that had been involved in our own otherworldly experiences.

It seemed Valerie had been gifted with a huge download of information relating to an ancient ETI genetic engineering program on this planet. Though the book does not offer much in the way of objective evidence to support the events described, we had our own reasons to suspect that it detailed actual occurrences from the remote past.

Before providing our validation of the accounts offered by Valerie Barrow, we must first introduce a little of her material. Though it is not essential to have read *ALCHE-RINGA . . . When the First Ancestors Were Created* before reading the remainder of this book, it certainly helps to have a copy available. I share only a basic overview and highlight the most spectacular claims. My focus is on those elements that I identified as being essential to validate.

Soon after the stone arrived, Valerie was woken from her sleep by a disembodied voice that asked her if she was ready to write a book. The conversation between Valerie and the discarnate voice continued over time, and she was informed that she was in communication with a star person (extraterrestrial) connected with the artifact. The entity referred to itself as Alcheringa and claimed that the object in the box was imbued with valuable information, brought to Earth almost nine hundred thousand years ago.

The Alcheringa being initially made itself known via a form of "voice to skull" communication. The communication was not audible but received telepathically. The experience would be like that of psychic mediumship, though there are technologies that emulate this communicative process. One team of researchers at MIT (Massachusetts Institute of Technology) has found a way to use lasers to direct information right into a person's ear. This is a photoacoustic effect, the result of material such as water vapor in the air absorbing light and forming sound waves. We can safely assume an advanced alien civilization will have moved far beyond such methods and found more direct means for communication, essentially synthetic telepathy.[8]

The object contained highly advanced intelligence, an "uploaded" aspect of consciousness, that we might think of as a post-biological entity. At a later stage, the entity stated that it was able to influence humans so that they would carry it around to locations it wanted to move to, using a very active form of subconscious psychic suggestion.

It seems quite logical to suspect that Alcheringa was the personality for an AI technology, functioning as a monitoring and recording sentinel until the appropriate moment for open contact had been reached by our species. It might even be that it encountered some prespecified electromagnetic frequency associated with our technological development.

Intuitive people (such as Daniella and I) are intimately familiar with this type of subliminal communication process. It is possible to psychically receive sensations, vivid imagery, or sudden, spontaneous "knowing." Once this powerful process of communication had been initiated, Valerie began to gain an enormous amount of information concerning an ancient extraterrestrial visitation to our planet.

Alcheringa explained to Valerie that she would soon start meeting people connected with the extraterrestrial mission. These other individuals would help to reveal the role this event had played in human origins. This prediction came to pass just as the entity said it would, with more than thirty people eventually providing relevant past life memories for the book *ALCHERINGA . . . When the First Ancestors Were Created.* Soon after communication began with Valerie, events began to unfold, with plenty of high strangeness.

One of Valerie's friends, Rachel, was driving with a respected Aboriginal healer, Gerry, near Valerie's house. At the mention of the particular Aboriginal name of the house, Gerry suggested that they make a visit. Valerie was somewhat surprised to meet Gerry, as she had not had much direct contact with Australia's indigenous peoples. That this visit coincided with receiving an Aboriginal sacred artifact seemed to her beyond coincidence.

While talking, Valerie had the sudden, strong sense that Gerry already knew she had the stone. She mentioned it, and he immediately snapped back that it was "men's business." It is true that churinga stones are directly handled only by initiated men in Aboriginal culture.

Once Valerie explained how the rock had come to her, and that it was kept wrapped up and safely secured in a box, Gerry seemed satisfied. Valerie's offer for Gerry to see the stone was quickly declined. He looked slightly scared by the thought of handling the object, even with it wrapped.

After some conversations about the Alcheringa stone, Gerry mentioned that one of his friends also had interactions with an unseen being that referred to itself as Alcheringa. He then suggested they all visit a sacred site with engraved hieroglyphs located near the town of Gosford, in New South Wales. Gerry asked Valerie to bring the artifact, as perhaps the voice of the stone would speak to them on site. Valerie agreed and immediately remembered that Alcheringa had told her that he would one day talk through her to an Aboriginal person.

Today the hieroglyphs engraved on a stone feature near Gosford have become somewhat famous, but things were not that way when Valerie visited the site more than twenty years ago. The rock bluff with these symbols is itself an Aboriginal site, irrespective of the exact provenance of the hieroglyphs. Many people consider the glyphs, most of which look Egyptian, to be a peculiar hoax—merely modern additions to an Aboriginal site. Witness accounts exist suggesting that some of the symbols are recent creations.

However, this hoax claim seems to readily account for only a proportion of the symbols.

Valerie visited the site for the first time accompanied by Gerry and her friend Karen. Their experiences were somewhat more intense and otherworldly even than my own. After touching the glyphs and then moving to a higher part of the rocky outcrop, Alcheringa spoke through Valerie and announced that he had known the three individuals for many lifetimes. The being continued, explaining that all those present had a direct connection to the star people. Alcheringa told them that many of the glyphs had been cut by extraterrestrial beings and that life-forms from numerous worlds had visited Earth over many millions of years. These visitations involved directly influencing the development of life on this planet. Before departing, Alcheringa mentioned that the glyphs would eventually help to awaken many people.

Gerry then led the trio to a point known as Whale Rock overlooking the Brisbane waters. As they arrived, they all began to feel quite peculiar. There was a rock feature that looked like a stone bed melted into a large boulder. This strange stone bed–like depression comfortably allowed one person to lie down. Gerry mentioned that in past times Aboriginal women used this as a birthing place, lying down as they entered labor. Karen promptly lay down within the depression and closed her eyes.

The trio shortly found themselves spontaneously shifting into an altered state of consciousness. They were no longer in their natural bodies, and the scene around them suggested it was not the present day. Their bodies were now strange alien forms with long slender limbs, light bluish-gray skin, and elongated heads.

Down below in the Bay of Brisbane, a crashed saucer-shaped craft was slowly sinking. Above the wrecked ship, another hovered in the air plucking survivors from the sea. Valerie noticed a pod of dolphins was even helping to push some of the floundering humanoids toward the shore.

This type of vivid experience is known as a spontaneous past life recall, or you might also have heard of it as a time slip. One moment we are here in the present, and the next we are a person living in another time. When Daniella and I corresponded with the head of the perceptual studies department at the University of Virginia, Dr. Bruce Greyson, he suggested the term *retrocognition* to describe Daniella's personal journeys into the past.

Such events have happened to many people, though they don't commonly involve extraterrestrial beings, and you can find many relevant books and articles on the subject. They are entirely immersive; you feel that this is a direct real-life experience that you are living, unlike a conventional memory. Having had such experiences, Daniella and I can both fully empathize with how Valerie and her friends would have felt. While in the other person's body, you also have access to their emotions, thoughts, and memories—not just the immediate sensory input. In past life therapy, a healing modality in which I am qualified, people can be deliberately taken through these types of experiences to resolve past life issues affecting their present day lives.

Valerie and her two companions experienced being marooned survivors from a mission to Earth. They were aware of a plan that had involved a collective of many benevolent nonhuman species. The stellar journey had begun in the Pleiades star cluster—even though the various species involved did not necessarily originate in that region of space. Two locations linked to the aliens came to Valerie's mind, one being Lyra and another that sounded somewhat like Altair. Residents of many planetary systems were understood to be involved. The ship had traveled from the Pleiades nebula, the location of the spatial anomaly, which provided the gateway to Earth.

After the shared experience had finished, Valerie pieced together everything she could from her companions, including information from a related dream Gerry had had years before. In Gerry's earlier dream states he had experienced being onboard the mothership as a surprise attack began, with warnings going off around him. In the panic, he managed to get his family off the endangered vessel. Gerry remembered that he had piloted a small saucer toward the earth's surface with others on board, but it crashed into the water near a small beach. In the spontaneous past life experience, Gerry had found himself inside the saucer again, pinned down by part of the damaged craft, slowly drowning. His two otherworldly experiences, one during sleep and another while awake, fitted together perfectly.

Later, Valerie communicated again with Alcheringa to help unravel more of the puzzling events. The story that emerged was that of a sizable crystalline craft, imbued with its own consciousness, carrying fifty thousand colonists from the Pleiades. The plan was to take control of the earth from its rather unpleasant rulers. Successful negotiation had already been completed. Earth would then function as an outpost for benevolent races keen on assisting with modifying the belief systems of negative-intentioned entities inhabiting the surrounding sector of space. Just before taking full control of Earth, the opposing force of more aggressive extraterrestrials had broken the agreement and launched a surprise attack. Only a handful of scout craft had made it safely down, carrying fewer than a hundred survivors to the planet's surface.

With their plans in tatters and now lacking the equipment to successfully colonize an environmentally hostile planet, the survivors came up with a new idea. If not for this disaster and the sudden need to revise their plans, modern humans might not exist.

I must admit to having had a particularly strong emotional reaction to Valerie Barrow's book, especially when it detailed the destruction of an alien mothership. It reminded me of a powerful past-life type experience that I went through during a personal shamanic journey in 2002. During the fully immersive experience, I found myself as a tall extraterrestrial humanoid with an elongated head and wearing a blue jumpsuit. I was piloting a small spacecraft toward Earth and was aware of several hostile craft in pursuit.

While still in this visionary state, I experienced an intense and painful knowing that a terrible disaster had claimed the lives of my comrades. These beings had come in peace to assist the earth. Almost all of them had died in flames, their ship destroyed in the inky blackness of space.

My experiences during this shamanic journey mesh with one part of the account given in Valerie's book. It turns out I am not the only person to recall piloting a spacecraft toward Earth after a surprise attack. This synchronistic past-life memory was yet another prompt for me to take the accounts shared in the Alcheringa book into serious consideration.

We visited Valerie Barrow and her husband, John, in December 2016. They were kind enough to host our family for lunch at their home. We knew from that meeting that Valerie is a lovely lady and a kindred spirit. It felt very comfortable to be sharing a conversation with her about our respective supernormal experiences. There was considerable common ground.

After our visit to Valerie, Daniella and I began to wonder whether it might be possible to track down any tangible evidence that could validate *ALCHERINGA . . . When the First Ancestors Were Created*. It occurred to us that, though there might not have been any supporting material evidence in the mid-1990s or even when the book was published in 2002, perhaps in the subsequent years the situation could have changed. Might advances in archaeology, geology, and biological sciences provide at least some supporting direct evidence?

Along with a small group of friends and family, I decided to start by visiting the Gosford Glyphs. It is indeed an odd place for anyone to plan a hoax, as ordinarily such things are done where they will be quickly heard about. Usually the purpose of such a deception would be to cause a big stir locally, providing the perpetrator with amusement. The location involved in this case is almost impossible to find by accident and hard even when you are looking for it. The engravings are well hidden within a large rocky outcrop and not at all visible even from the small path that winds its way through the surrounding forest.

The only prominent marker for the site is a giant eucalyptus tree, known locally as the grandmother tree. Some climbing is required to reach the small crevasse in which the symbols themselves are on display. Daniella is not a great fan of clambering around on slippery rocks, so she limited herself to peering down at them from a vantage point above, leaving our young son and me to do the monkey business of clambering in and taking photos.

While Daniella remained alone, she took some time to tune in to the energy of the place and soon had the strong impression that she was in the women's business part of the site and that men should be on the other side. Shortly after this, she noticed a humanoid figure that approached. She felt it was the caretaker spirit for the place. The entity checked her out and then headed toward where the rest of us were examining the engravings. Daniella was a little worried that the entity might not be happy with people being there, but nothing negative happened to anyone.

Daniella looked toward the grandmother tree and instantly felt the presence of three female elders sitting around her. They started talking about the "time before there was time." They explained the purpose of the site, which is divided among healing, storytelling, and interdimensional travel. The spirit women started to sing or hum a tune, and then a light rain began to fall. It felt very peaceful, and Daniella's sense was of having returned to the site after being there long ago. When Daniella started to carefully make her way back down the slippery rocks, another female spirit emerged and guided her down so that she would not fall. She also had a familiar feel, as though there was some level of kinship. There were moments where it felt as though she was holding Daniella steady. It was all very vivid.

Meanwhile, where I was with the rest of our group, some people were suggesting they felt a strong sense of alien connection to the glyphs. I make no claims myself, as I feel that, until they are shown to be ancient, there is little point in me going further than saying that I feel Kariong is a very special and important Aboriginal site—a place where long ago beings from the dreaming walked the earth.

CHAPTER 7

PAST LIFE MEMORIES
AND ALIEN MESSAGES

*The wish not to believe, can influence as
strongly as the wish to believe.*

—DR. IAN STEVENSON, psychiatrist
and reincarnation researcher

E ach further communication with the artifact added more
to the story of the mission from the Pleiades and the survivors marooned on Earth. Over the months that followed,
Valerie Barrow encountered well more than twenty people
who shared past life memories of the same series of events.
These people and their strange recollections further corrob-
orated details included in Alcheringa's transmissions. Some
of the witnesses had previously experienced dreams about
the mission, but most only recalled their past life memories
once shown photographs of the glyphs at Gosford.

As more of the story emerged, it was revealed that the
surviving star people decided that the only way they could
still positively change Earth's future was by passing on
their mission objectives to an appropriate creature already
suited to life on the planet. They selected an upright, hairy

ape-man they had encountered, and then the genetic engineering began.

The new modified and hybridized being would, in time, be suitable for the dying star people themselves to incarnate into as required. This is a form of directed reincarnation, as used by some Tibetan Buddhist masters.[1] It was also intended that the new beings would serve as biological containers for the souls of other less-pleasant cosmic entities. This latter consideration was deemed essential.

The new creature had spiritual potential beyond that of the local galactic intelligence, which was stuck in a shallow level of consciousness. Incarnation into the newly modified hominin would provide a path of spiritual progression for various negative entities—a chance for these species to evolve toward higher states of consciousness.

You might wonder why allied forces did not simply send any rescue attempt. In fact, a fleet of ships arrived five years after the attack. By the time this flotilla of craft reached Earth, many more of the marooned star people had died, primarily due to their being incredibly poorly suited to the earth's environment.

Everything around them was hostile to the aliens: the intense solar radiation, waterborne bacteria, airborne viruses, and poisonous plants all claimed victims. Without all the advanced technologies carried on the mothership, colonization was utterly impossible. Even genetic engineering had been a struggle with the limited supplies and medical equipment that had been recovered.

The few beings who remained alive were by now committed to helping upgrade the local hominin species. Almost all these survivors declined the offer of rescue and continued working on creating the new human form. One member of their party, a crystalline entity housed in a robotic containment suit, had been essential to the work due to its incredible sensitivities and capabilities.

The crews of these newly arrived ships were not colonists. They were a warrior race of a feline humanoid species (leonine people). The battle group commander issued a final decree to all remaining enemy forces hidden in their underground caverns: vacate the planet immediately or face the full force of alliance retribution. Though most of the hostile forces soon withdrew, heading through a gateway to Orion, some refused. The subsequent aerial bombardment of their strongholds was swift and decisive.

I could never hope to validate many of the intricate details that emerged from Valerie's interaction with the artifact and her conversations with those that had past life memories. That does not mean they are not accurate or can't perhaps be proven accurate at some later stage.

What felt vital to me was an analysis of the most significant claim: that aliens came to Earth and helped to direct human evolution. Eventually, I identified a few hugely substantial details in the narrative and selected a handful of critical events that could confirm the visitation. Before going any further let's quickly summarize my target list:

- Provide evidence supporting the claim that Earth was seeded with DNA by an advanced galactic civilization several billion years ago.

- Provide evidence supporting the claim that extraterrestrial beings could possess technologies capable of traveling across the universe and even through time.

- Provide material evidence proving that a vast crystalline spacecraft exploded in orbit above Australia.

- Provide geological proof that Earth was deliberately bombarded by asteroids as part of a Pleiadian reprisal for the ambush of their colonists.

- Provide climatic data supporting the claimed severity of the impact of the extraterrestrial reprisals stated to have occurred five years after the ambush.

- Provide detailed genetic information from academic sources that represents evidence of deliberate engineering of ancestral *Homo sapiens*.

- Provide a scientifically well-supported analysis of the impact and implications of the specific modification made to create ancestral *Homo sapiens*.

I freely admit that this initially sounded like an impossibly ambitious list. I realized there was an additional factor to consider: timing. This investigation required one further fixed constraint. All the scientific evidence uncovered needed to point to the same singular period to be considered valid supportive data.

We had an approximate target date for the events of nine hundred thousand years ago, but I knew from my involvement with psychical research that this might be more of a general guide than a fixed point. Obtaining precise dates from information acquired through higher dimensions outside of our linear space-time continuum is a tricky affair. That said, this dating had come up several times in *ALCHERINGA . . . When the First Ancestors Were Created*, so my thought was that even if the ETI measured the time somewhat differently or the length of a year had somehow changed, it shouldn't be off by hundreds of thousands of years.

For the purposes of our research project, we took nine hundred thousand years ago as the central point and began looking at data spanning from one million to eight hundred thousand years ago. (As it would later turn out, had we not used this more expansive range in our protocol we would have failed to find any proof.)

I am sure that some readers will struggle with the idea that a sacred Aboriginal artifact could carry the interactive consciousness of an extraterrestrial being. For those same people, I imagine that it will also be hard to accept anyone can re-experience events from the distant past. Keep in mind that the validity of these sources can be established by any success resulting from relying upon them. They are either self-validating or self-debunking in this context.

Many highly qualified scientists and philosophers have pondered what to expect from highly advanced extraterrestrial civilizations. We encountered some excellent examples of what alien technologies might be like in our earlier investigations. Susan Schneider, a prominent neuroscientist at the University of Pennsylvania, has published some of her thoughts on this matter. Schneider agrees with other notable people we have encountered in believing that advanced beings will likely have transitioned to a post-biological existence. This might be uploading their minds into silicon-based networks or even something stranger such as a noncorporeal existence. Some entities may also be merged with the very fabric of reality itself.[2]

Not to labor the point, but even biological entities will likely send a probe ahead of any physical visitation to our planet. It would probably be challenging for us to even recognize some types of extraterrestrial visitors or their information-processing technologies. It is not at all strange to think one might be so well camouflaged that it just looks like some old rock to us.

As for the validity of so-called past life memories as a source of information, substantial scientific evidence for this has been available for several decades. Professor Ian Stevenson of the University of Virginia's Division of Perceptual Studies conducted detailed academic research into children's memories of recent past lives. Over some forty years, Stevenson was able to track down places, people, and events that perfectly matched the stories given to him in hundreds of cases. These experiencers were usually very young children with little knowledge of the wider world. Under rigid scientific protocols, a respected and skeptical academic (along with the various international scientists who assisted him) concluded that past life memories genuinely produced historically accurate information in many cases. No matter the exact functioning of the reincarnation process itself or whatever mechanisms caused it to occur, that there was a real underlying phenomenon is made clear.

For anyone wanting to look more into the evidence of past life memories providing verifiable data, I recommend exploring Stevenson's vast body of work. The veritable treasure trove of research includes about three hundred papers and fourteen books. Stevenson's most exceptional work is the 2,268-page, two-volume *Reincarnation and Biology: A Contribution to the Etiology of Birthmarks and Birth Defects* (1997). Consider that this masterwork incorporated two hundred cases of birthmarks and birth defects that corresponded to wounds on the deceased person whose life the child recalled. Having read several of his investigative reports, I can refer to them only as stunning and utterly convincing.

Stevenson is not the only scientist or medical professional to stumble into the field of past life memories and uncover the potential for them to provide detailed accounts of long-distant events. In 1962, a highly respected English psychiatrist named Dr. Arthur Guirdham was visited by a female patient, Mrs. Smith, who was haunted by vivid and violent nightmares. Her terrible dreams seemed to center on some period in ancient history that she could not consciously place.

As Smith shared names, details, and historical information from her recurrent nocturnal journeys, Guirdham recognized clear links to the Cathars and to the Catholic crusades that eradicated them. The Cathars were considered Christian heretics, at least in the eyes of the Catholic Church. Eventually, the Inquisition arranged for a bloody invasion of their lands, ending in a final, barbaric massacre of the surviving men, women, and children at Montségur in 1244.

The high strangeness had only just begun; the respected psychiatrist, a graduate from the prestigious Oxford University, was about to find himself at the center of one of the century's most stunning reincarnation cases.

Soon after Smith opened up about her troubling visions, several more of Guirdham's female patients began detailing similar flashbacks. Eventually, he came to suspect that he was at the center of something almost unheard of: a case of mass reincarnation. All these patients lived within about fifteen miles of the city of Bristol.

Guirdham found that he was also able to recall memories that suggested he had a link to Smith and the events she described. He set out to unravel the truth of the matter and sifted through all available historical sources. In time, Guirdham successfully identified about a dozen of the names offered to him by his patients. Keep in mind that most of these names linked to unremarkable persons of the thirteenth century and could not have been known of by these patients.[3]

In fact, it took a skilled search through ancient records, helped by reputable historians, to locate these former incarnations listed among the records of the French Inquisition. This is hardly a source regularly visited by members of the public. I am sure most of us would have no idea such records even existed.

It is worth taking a moment here to highlight some exciting overlaps between Guirdham's story and our own. Among these is the fact that Daniella and I both consider ourselves to be Gnostic thinkers, as were the Cathars. Daniella's grandfather once told her that their family's ancestry traced back to the Cathars in Southern France. Also, I grew up about a thirty-minute drive northeast from where Guirdham's clinic had been and not far from the area where the patients had lived.

Perhaps the most notable connection between these two cases of what seems to be group reincarnation is the fact that Valerie Barrow has herself written about a remembered life as a Cathar initiate, one of those that burned at Montségur.

This additional past life account features in her book *Two Soulmates: Walking Through Time & History* (2013). It seems an astonishing coincidence that there are direct connections between the two instances of mass reincarnation, with one occurring in England, from which both Valerie's husband, John, and I both originate, and the other in Australia, where both Valerie and Daniella were born.

Reincarnation is part of various philosophical and spiritual collectives, most famously the Hindus and Buddhists, but it is also a feature of many shamanic traditions and accepted by Gnostics, Celts, and Druse, among many others. Collective group reincarnations seem to suggest that there is some other level of order in specific instances of rebirth, perhaps a consciously direct element in which some people can choose where, when, and with whom they will be reborn.

Tibetan Buddhist masters have long claimed that, due to their advanced meditation practices, it is possible for them to choose the specific details of their next life and even select the moment of departure. Research into this process, which involves numerous tests to identify returned Buddhist masters, seems to suggest this really does happen.

Even though I am supportive of reincarnation being the best explanation for why many people remember details from lives in the far past, we must keep in mind that we are exploring a rather exceptional instance of retrocognition. This is an instance of humans remembering lives as advanced alien entities. It would be wrong of me to ignore the possibility that other explanations exist for these astonishing memories. We will quickly consider an additional three potential scenarios that might explain, or play some role in, the retrieval of these strange alien memories.

A growing number of neuroscientists and geophysicists are intrigued by the relationship between the workings of the human brain and the electromagnetic field of the planet.

Experimental results support the existence of a magnetosensory system in humans, akin to that of other animals. In March 2019 a study involving thirty-four participants revealed geomagnetic stimulation could initiate a decrease in amplitude of EEG alpha oscillations (8–13 Hz) occurring in a repeatable manner. Such a response is typically associated with changes in sensory and cognitive processing of external stimuli such as sounds and images. There was, however, no conscious awareness of the field changes recognized by the subjects. Why humans possess magnetosensory sensitivity only as an unconscious "ability" remained mysterious.[4]

In a recent article for the Scientific and Medical Network, geophysicist Paul Kieniewicz discusses the ongoing research into the way our brains might be interacting with natural Earth energies. Kieniewicz explains that in the space between the earth's surface and the ionosphere is a cavity enclosing the earth's electromagnetic field. In this space, extremely low frequencies exist that form standing waves. These electrical and magnetic standing waves are continually energized by lightning strikes and have resonant peaks at 8 Hz, 14 Hz, 21 Hz, and 27 Hz. These resonant peaks are best known as Schumann resonances.[5]

Neurologists have noticed that the electrical fields within the Schumann resonances often match those of the human brain. Eminent physical neuroscientist Michael Persinger and several of his associates had even suggested that there could be information transferring back and forth between the human brain and the earth's field.[6] This information may be carried in the form of light produced by living organisms known as biophotons. Indeed, such light photons are even emitted from DNA itself.

Kieniewicz leaves us with the question of whether the earth's field could store human thoughts, just as our brain stores these as memories, allowing other individuals to reach into that field and retrieve them. The next time you have a strange dream, perhaps consider whether it was received from these standing waves, because while we are in a deep sleep, our brain patterns tend to resonate with the earth's field, making us potentially more susceptible to such information transfer. Might it be possible that we can access the experiences of beings that lived on Earth in the distant past, even those of alien creatures that arrived here hundreds of thousands of years ago?

Another peculiar mode of memory storage is known as genetic memory. This concerns memories present at birth that exist in the absence of sensory experience. Ordinarily, such memories become incorporated into the genome over long periods of time. We can think of the programmed automatic behavior of newborn babies in this category. The emerging field of epigenetics has revealed that life experiences, though not directly coded in human DNA, can be passed on to children. Studies have shown that traumatic events may have effects on subsequent generations. Our experiences change how genes express themselves, and this genetic expression can then be inherited.

There is growing interest in the capacity of DNA to store memories. That DNA can record many forms of information is no secret. Researchers have even come up with a way to encode digital data in DNA. If we were to use DNA to hold our data records, it would provide the highest-density large-scale data storage method ever. Consider that it is calculated we can potentially store around 215 million gigabytes of data per gram of DNA.[7] But what about vivid human memories? Can these also be written directly to our DNA molecules?

Famous psychologist Carl Jung theorized that we're born with the memories and experiences of our ancestors imprinted into our DNA. This might at first sound a bit hard to swallow, but cutting-edge research is beginning to support Jung's theory. We know today that at least some of the experiences our ancestors went through are providing us with direct knowing today. We call this instinctive behavior. If specific traumas have passed on warnings to us at an unconscious level, via inherited DNA, might there be far more information stored away that we are just not accessing, or that we are only interacting with at an unconscious level?

Professor Berit Brogaard, a University of Miami philosopher specializing in the areas of cognitive neuroscience and philosophy of mind, suspects that we may at least be able to tap into specific skills that ancestors had, perhaps a talent for a musical instrument or a gift for mathematics.[8]

While Brogaard remains skeptical as to whether we can hope to access fully immersive memories of specific past events, she acknowledges that there is much we do not yet know about the brain.

It might be possible that essential memories from our first ancestors can be accessed from our DNA—not just memories but also any unique gifts they had—which is profoundly important considering we are talking about powerfully psychic extraterrestrial beings.

The third scenario has to do with advanced extraterrestrial science. The famous futurist Arthur C. Clarke is known for one quote in particular: "Any sufficiently advanced technology is indistinguishable from magic."[9] We must try to appreciate the difference between technology as we understand it and as it may be wielded by members of an advanced alien civilization.

Professor Paul Davies suggests that some extraterrestrial technologies will be non-physical, undetectable, or unrecognizable as functional technology.[10] We really do not know the limitations of what highly advanced entities could do to our mental processes remotely.

Evidence of beings far in advance of us, perhaps by millions of years, would include technologies bordering on magical and unthinkable. The peculiar leaf-wrapped object that came into Valerie's custodianship could be designed to record events and beam data and images into human minds.

It could possibly be that transmissions from the object give recipients the impression of reliving the experiences of the long-dead extraterrestrial beings, passing on crucial detailed information by this method. It certainly stands out to me that it would be ingenious to suitably camouflage an advanced technology when it is intended for use on a low-tech planet.

CHAPTER 8

EXOGENESIS AND THE SEEDING OF EARTH

Contrary to the popular notion that only creationism
relies on the supernatural, evolutionism must as well,
since the probabilities of random formation of life
are so tiny as to require a "miracle" for spontaneous
generation tantamount to a theological argument.

—PROFESSOR CHANDRA WICKRAMASINGHE,
astrobiologist

We previously encountered a global survey by Glocalities that investigated belief in alien life among 26,492 people from twenty-four countries. This survey found that 25 percent of respondents believed that the first form of life on Earth arrived here from another place in the universe.[1] This is not so surprising when we consider biological life on our planet is posited to have emerged from geological and chemical processes, and yet we have no model for how that can happen.

In 2013, academic researchers Maxim Makukov, PhD, and Vladimir Shcherbak, PhD, published "The 'Wow! Signal' of the Terrestrial Genetic Code." The paper detailed evidence that the human genome contains genetic material designed by an advanced alien civilization. These two scientists should be well qualified to judge, having spent thirteen years working on the mapping of human DNA for the Human Genome Project. Makukov and Shcherbak discovered patterns in our DNA code suggestive of alien progenitors wanting to preserve a complex message. The scientific duo suspected that these aliens had created DNA to seed life on other planets. They also suspected that much of the 97 percent of noncoding sequences in human DNA included genetic code that could be associated with various alien life-forms.[2]

Following initial criticisms of their work, Makukov and Shcherbak conducted further investigations. This led to a second paper in which they determined that the structure of the genetic code is consistent with the hypothesis that an alien message has been encoded. Their view is that the structure of the encoding makes sense from a SETI perspective, as it includes the "zero-based positional notation, encoded in the direction from codons to amino acids" and "the notion of zero as a number in its own right, encoded explicitly in the opposite direction from amino acids to codons," and their conclusion is that the observed findings are sufficient to be considered a message that can be read as "to whom it may concern, we were here."[3]

This suggestion meshes well with information that Alcheringa provided, suggesting that our DNA carries code from various extraterrestrial species. Earth apparently considered to be a kind of living library, recording the code for life-forms existing across the universe. The Human Genome Project scientists reached the conclusion that humans were designed only after stumbling on a "set of arithmetic patterns and ideographic symbolic language" encoded into our DNA.[4]

This is not the first time that respected scientists have pointed to an alien origin for life on this planet. One of the co-discoverers of the double helix structure of DNA, Francis Crick, found the existence of DNA to be such an unlikely affair that he suggested it was reasonable to suspect that the first life on Earth was deliberately seeded by an advanced intelligence. The complexity of the DNA code makes it hard to fathom how it could emerge out of some dirt and elementary chemicals swirling about in a primeval rock pool. Even if we allowed for a vast period to pass, it is debatable whether DNA could ever spontaneously emerge. This skeptical position is shared by many scientists.[5]

One glaring anomaly is that it did not take life an extensive period to appear on Earth. Our planet formed as a fireball of magma and hot toxic gases around 4.6 billion years ago. Close to 4.5 billion years ago a thin crust began to build amid an ongoing meteoric bombardment. Despite this inhospitable environment, the first evidence of fossil life has been found in Canadian rock formations dated to 4.2 billion years. The fossil discovery in Canada led scientists to speculate that life may have emerged on Earth as early as 4.5 billion years ago, almost as soon as there was a crust.[6] This deduction for life's early emergence was later confirmed by a team of researchers from the University of Bristol (in the UK) led by Davide Pisane. The scientists used twenty-nine DNA codes common to various species so that they could identify the last universal common ancestor of life (LUCA) and arrived at the same dating hypothesis: 4.5 billion years ago.[7] It begins to sound as if the seeds of life were already in place merely waiting for the right conditions for them to germinate.

This is precisely the model favored by Crick and other academics, such as Chandra Wickramasinghe, a highly respected astrobiologist known for advocating panspermia, life originating from microorganisms or chemical precursors present in outer space. (The term *panspermia* is interchangeable with *exogenesis*.) Molecules raining down from the cosmos then spontaneously initiate organic growth once in a suitable environment. Panspermia-based models sometimes suggest that the precursors of life might drift through the cosmos inside comets. Directed panspermia refers to life being deliberately sent by advanced civilizations.

In the 1972 paper "Directed Panspermia," Francis Crick remarks on the likelihood of life coming from space, "The time available makes it possible, therefore, that technological societies existed elsewhere in the galaxy even before the formation of the Earth. We should, therefore, consider a new 'infective' theory, namely that a primitive form of life was deliberately planted on the Earth by a technologically advanced society on another planet."[8]

Crick reminds us that the DNA molecule is responsible for all life on this planet. There were not multiple events that gave rise to life on Earth, as one would expect if emergence was chaotic and random. If life could potentially happen spontaneously anywhere at any time, why do we instead have evidence that all life began with the same single-celled organisms based on identical DNA strands?

Life emerged once only, from there it quickly took root, and that unique process gave rise to all the life-forms we know to have existed. There is no evidence to suggest that in the subsequent 4.5 billion years chemical processes ever again produced biological organisms.

There is nothing unreasonable in the idea that intelligent races might choose to seed barren planets, perhaps seeking to terraform them for their later use or just to ensure the continuance of their genetic code were there a localized extinction event.

Alternatively, the dispersal of life across the galaxy might represent a long-duration scientific experiment. If that latter suggestion reflects reality, it might also mean extraterrestrial entities would take an interest in the process of evolution as it occurs on planets they have seeded. We might expect these entities to be visiting developing worlds to monitor or redirect some part of their experiment.

If Earth is a cosmic petri dish, it may be that various significant events throughout our evolutionary history were directed rather than merely occurring through the workings of chance. Several key moments in evolutionary history have been highlighted as being rather anomalous.

Direct discoveries have supported the idea aliens are sending the seeds of life out into space, with some of these reaching our planet in more recent times. In early 2015, microbiologist Milton Wainwright, PhD, announced that his team had recovered a minuscule sphere composed of a titanium-vanadium alloy from sixteen miles up in the earth's upper atmosphere. The tiny object had impacted their sampling device at high speed and was leaking a strange organic goo.[9] It should be noted that vanadium is rarely found in its metallic form in nature and that when used in small amounts with other metals it creates incredibly strong alloys. Wainwright tentatively suggested that this object might be a mechanism used by some unknown extraterrestrial species to seed life into the cosmos.[10]

Wickramasinghe and Wainwright are among many scientists who have demonstrated that microorganisms can be carried to Earth by fragmented comets and may potentially give rise to viral outbreaks among human populations. There is already startling evidence that rains of extraterrestrial material from the stratosphere may link to the sudden emergence of new forms of sickness in populations. Whether genetic material from space is directly the cause or provokes mutations in existing viruses remains a matter of some debate. Growing numbers of scientists are calling for this issue of viral rain to be taken more seriously.

Professor Edward Steele, biologist and immunologist at the CY O'Connor ERADE Village Foundation in Australia, explains there has been a growing recognition that horizontal gene transfer plays a key role in evolution. The agency largely responsible is cross-species infection by viruses. Steele feels that horizontal gene transfer is associated with panspermia and that the transfer of genetic information is coming from sources well beyond our planet's biosphere.

When we consider the vast number of habitable worlds in our galaxy, panspermia could allow for all kinds of organisms to be spread among systems. Gradually the evidence for microorganisms raining down onto our planet from space has been growing. Steele warns that "ignoring this possibility of a continuing input of microbial and viral genes to the Earth from the external universe might be fraught with imminent danger."[11]

Viruses and cells have been coevolving with terrestrial organisms since life arose on the planet. Cells evolving to resist their viral invaders can give rise to new forms and behaviors as viruses move genes between unrelated cells. Scientists call this process horizontal gene transfer (HGT).

HGT explains the presence of genes discovered within organisms that don't come from any direct ancestor. Such genes can come from a separate animal species or a microorganism. This process has played a significant role in creating the tremendous diversity of life on Earth, with viruses and bacteria carrying new code into the genomes of most organisms.[12]

At present, there are at least 145 functional genes in the human genome that have arrived relatively recently from other species, including bacteria, fungi, plants, and animals. In humans, HGT-derived genes are most commonly found to code for regulation of the immune response system and tend to offer less-than-apparent advantages to the organism. Some of the HGT genes are even involved in determining our blood type, a rather intriguing fact, especially as many people find that blood types seem to correlate with unusual personal traits.

Vast clouds of viral genetic information are literally raining down from the atmosphere, provoking evolutionary modifications. This continual flow of genetic data among species may be the key driver for the ongoing emergence of novelty in well-established biological systems. This infective process may be more critical (certainly much faster) in impact than random mutations and natural section.

A recent study on the cause of the Cambrian explosion found compelling evidence for the involvement of retroviruses that arrived from space. Incredibly, it seems that emergence of the complex retroviruses of the vertebrate lines coincides with this rapid acceleration in evolutionary change and species diversification five hundred million years ago.

The same study also found various anomalies in the unique evolution of the highly intelligent octopus. Features such as a large brain, sophisticated nervous system, camera-like eyes, flexible body, and instantaneous camouflage via the ability to switch color and shape, among other astonishing traits, emerged suspiciously suddenly in evolutionary terms.

The genes that would give rise to these traits seem to be missing from any conceivable ancestral species and instead suggested to the scientists they were either "borrowed" from some future evolutionary event or must come from elsewhere in the cosmos. Could an alien-engineered retrovirus have carried the essential genes from some distant extraterrestrial species?

The scientists go even further and ponder whether the frozen, fertilized octopus eggs might have arrived on Earth in a comet 270 million years ago. I would suggest a more logical deduction is that the octopus was genetically modified in situ by intelligent visitors. If anything, the "comet" seems to be an academic placeholder for the more viable suggestion that an alien craft brought the eggs to our planet. I imagine these scientists are understandably worried that any talk of visiting extraterrestrial intelligence will make them targets of media attacks. A comet carrying frozen octopus eggs across the cosmos just seems so strangely unreasonable in comparison to the more viable delivery method of a structured craft.

It must be noted that the octopus is far from the only creature that is best explained in the fossil record as an arrival from space or genetic engineering in situ. Indeed, it is suggested in the same paper that most major life-forms could be better explained with the revised panspermia-based model. According to the article "Cause of Cambrian Explosion—Terrestrial or Cosmic?" (2018): "Many of these 'unearthly' properties of organisms can be plausibly explained if we admit the enlarged cosmic biosphere that is indicated by modern astronomical research—discoveries of exoplanets already discussed. The average distance between habitable planets in our galaxy now to be reckoned in light years—typically 5 light years."[13]

Viruses code their genetic information using both RNA and DNA, in single- and double-stranded forms. Cellular life uses double-stranded DNA only. This fact led some scientists to suspect that viruses represent descendants of ancient life-forms that lived before DNA existed. The DNA molecule is incapable of building itself; it is reliant on proteins. The process for proteins to order correctly is reliant on the information contained within DNA. We have here a molecular process requiring the synthesis of two distinct complex systems. They must emerge together. When we come to consider the mathematical probability of even one single protein arising, things quickly become mind boggling.

Each protein is constructed from a selection of twenty amino acids, strung together in a precise order to form a chain of two hundred. There is a one in 10^{260} chance of the correct configuration by random process alone. This number is higher than the total of all atoms in the observable universe.

Francis Crick eventually settled on the opinion that it was not feasible that this high level of complexity at the cellular level could have arisen by chance. Especially dubious was that such complexity could emerge in so short a period as it did on Earth, which we now know to be a mere one hundred thousand years.

This does not mean all life in the universe had the same odds stacked against its emergence. We really don't even know if all life is based on the DNA molecule. It might be that organisms emerged first in a very different way and with a distinct foundation. Beings produced from this alternative emergence event may have then later created the DNA molecule as a terraforming technology (intended to modify planetary environments).

It certainly feels unreasonable for such a system to emerge spontaneously, being reliant on two highly complex molecular processes and an intricate language structure with four nucleobases. These nucleobases—guanine, thymine, cytosine, and adenine—combine with twenty amino acids. There also needs to be a translation mechanism, and the proteins themselves are coded in the language of DNA.

It seems counterintuitive that while life continually evolves, DNA's functionality and the code remained entirely unchanged. The summary here is that DNA appears to emerge improbably fast, is mind-bogglingly complex, initiated in its perfected form, and remains constant and stable in functionality almost indefinitely.

The suggestion that DNA was seeded on Earth would allow for life having emerged over a much more extended period, just not initially on this planet in what is, in cosmic or even geological terms, the blink of an eye. Life may have begun with organisms not based on DNA at all, or something else similar, but that DNA has been designed by advanced civilizations as a method to terraform new worlds. The DNA code offers almost infinite possibilities with respect to the organisms it can build and the environments it can shape life toward.

Alcheringa had explained to Valerie that Earth had been seeded with life by extraterrestrial beings several billion years before the mothership traveled to the planet. In fact, it was the productive potential of the DNA molecule at the base of all life on our planet that had drawn the attention of several rather unpleasant species, eventually resulting in them annexing Earth.

These rather unpleasant entities had wanted access to the living library of intergalactic genetic codes. The new owners of Earth then used their genetic sciences to create creatures that benefited them or provided amusement. One of the new species engineered by the invaders was the very first hominin, a distant ancestor of modern humans.

Significant numbers of psychics and shamans have also been given the information that Earth was seeded by extraterrestrial beings. In modern times, well-known American psychic channel Barbara Marciniak has written several books in which she shares her understanding that DNA was sent here by entities referred to as "the planners." These planners explained to her, through psychic communication, that the earth is a living library storing the genetic code from a wide range of galactic species. This is precise, as Alcheringa explained to Valerie.

One famous anthropologist turned shamanic practitioner, Michael Harner, PhD, describes a relevant visionary experience he had with the Amazonian psychedelic brew ayahuasca. During the visions, Harner was shown strange dragon-like creatures falling down to Earth from space. These entities informed him they had escaped pursuit by enemies out in the cosmos. The aliens then showed him how they had created life on early Earth to disguise their presence, hiding within their own creations (humans). Later, Harner realized that the reference to these creatures hiding within all life might refer to the DNA molecule itself, being that this is inside all organisms.

The beings considered themselves masters of the planet and that humans were but receptacles and servants. The communication between them seemed to be coming to him from the lower part of his brain, known as the reptilian brain stem—the most primitive part of the human neurological system.[14] This description immediately reminded me of a race of aliens Alcheringa referred to as the Draco. These Draco are malevolent, winged, reptilian-like entities and are explained to be the original enemy of the alien alliance he was associated with (prompting the alliance to form).

Harner went on to describe his experience to a respected Conibo shaman, and this man recognized the entities described and dismissed their claim over the earth, clarifying that they were only the "masters of outer darkness" as he pointed up to the sky.[15] Harner had not mentioned the fact that the entities had dropped down from space and was considerably freaked out.

Later, a local evangelist missionary that he spoke to about the visions highlighted the story of Satan's defeat by archangel Michael. Within the story a war in heaven is described after which the dragon and his angels were cast down to Earth. They then went on to deceive the whole world. Harner, an atheist, was left stunned by the apparent overlaps in the biblical narrative and his shamanic experience.[16]

Though there is substantial evidence that DNA was seeded on Earth by advanced extraterrestrial civilizations, scientific data also suggests that *Homo sapiens* are not only the distant descendants of spores delivered to this planet but were more recently directly engineered from a terrestrial creature by visitors to this world. We explore that evidence in a later chapter. First, we need to understand how extraterrestrial entities might be able to travel to our planet.

CHAPTER 9

WARP DRIVES AND WORMHOLES

If the black hole like Sagittarius A, located
at the centre of our own galaxy, is large and
rotating, then the outlook for a spacecraft changes
dramatically. That's because the singularity that a
spacecraft would have to contend with is very gentle
and could allow for a very peaceful passage.*

—PROFESSOR GAURAV KHANNA, physicist

For extraterrestrial entities to take any role in Earth's prehistory, they would require advanced technologies far
beyond anything humans possess today, or at least well
beyond anything visible to us in public. I can't offer conclu-
sive evidence of how aliens reached Earth, though we can
at least explore the feasibility of ancient visitations to our
planet based on a look at known and theoretical space travel
technologies.

My generation grew up in what has been termed the space
age. I was born a year after *Viking 1* sent the first images of
Mars back to Earth and have lived through a range of subsequent developments, including successful artificial probe

missions to all the local planetary systems. Until recently humanity has been limited to rocket technology, which has proven inadequate to allow for direct human exploration of the planets in our solar system. The moon has been our only success story until today.

In just the last couple of years, NASA has been testing a new drive system, known as the EM drive. This has caused a lot of heated debate among physicists, as it seems to break the accepted rules by producing thrust without burning fuel. Some calculations suggest that if the EM drive works as hoped it might take astronauts to Mars in as little as seventy days. The Chinese government claims to already have a working prototype of this propulsion system, and other parties are planning their own tests for this new technology.[1]

Scientists are also investigating the potential of nuclear thermal and nuclear electric propulsion systems. These could take us to Proxima Centauri (4.24 light-years away) in about one thousand years. Compare this capability to the currently utilized electronic ion drive system, using accelerated ions for thrust, which requires an eighty-one-thousand-year journey to the same star system.

Several theoretical propulsion systems can potentially accelerate our journeys through space, including nuclear pulse propulsion, fusion rockets, fusion ramjet, laser sails, and antimatter engines. Unfortunately, for now, all these systems are hindered by a wide range of technical problems. In some cases, we would need an enormous craft with vast reserves of highly specialized fuel. In others, the construction costs equal more money than ever available or energy beyond the output of the entire planet. That is not to say they might not be feasible in the future as human technology reaches a far higher level.[2]

Two theoretical technologies sound as if they might be directly linked to Alcheringa's narrative. A description of how the mothership moves might suggest something like an Alcubierre drive: "We don't move into the gateway, we are suddenly just through it. There is no linear movement as such, we are just instantly there."[3]

The Alcubierre drive is close to the warp drive systems portrayed in the television show *Star Trek*. This technology creates a bubble in the time-space continuum in which the craft sits protected while space is warped to move around it, bringing the destination to the ship rather than the other way around. As the spacecraft is not being propelled forward, specific issues concerning time dilation (differences in the passage of time due to velocity) can be avoided. The other interesting point is that, though the passengers would reach their destination quicker than if traveling at light speed, the craft never itself breaks the speed of light (conserving the laws of physics).

This warp drive system would bring two points closer together. At least one source I explored suggested that an Alcubierre drive would allow a journey to Proxima Centauri in a mere four years, though other scientists consider that suggestion to be a conservative estimate. I asked for an opinion on this drive system from William Brown, the lead physicist at the Resonance Science Foundation. Brown was willing to offer a detailed summary of the workings and potential capabilities of the warp drive system. In his opinion, there is really no limit to how quickly you can arrive at your destination. Because you are warping both space and time (the space-time continuum), this technology becomes time travel by default.

By reducing the distance between two points, pulling the two points together, there is also a drastic change in the passage of time associated with any voyage due to relativity. The passengers aboard any craft using Alcubierre drive systems would necessarily be arriving in the past of the destination point (relative to the present time of the departure point). This sounds very strange (because it is), but remember, you are not just warping physical space but the space-time continuum, buckling the quantum substructure of the universe.

Though there is no doubt that an Alcubierre drive would be well suited for carrying beings from the Pleiades to Earth, there are some reasons to question if this system was used in the story we are exploring.

Valerie Barrow's information refers to a gateway as part of the system that brought the craft to our planet. This strongly suggests a different form of theoretical travel. She writes in *ALCHERINGA . . . When the First Ancestors Were Created:* "We are moving towards this energy pattern. It is a gateway. The gateway has two spiralling forms, and we are waiting for the right time to move into them."[4]

Brown explains that when you contract space-time beyond a certain degree, this creates a wormhole. This is the "ultimate transportation mechanism" because it joins point A to point B. This allows a journey in which there is no linear movement; rather than taking any time, you are just instantly there.[5]

What exactly is a wormhole and how could beings travel the universe with them?

Just a little more than a century ago, Austrian physicist Ludwig Flamm realized that the equations for the theory of relativity allowed for the existence of *white holes*, a kind of time reversal of black holes. Entrances to either a black or white hole could potentially be connected via a space-time conduit. This solution to the theoretical math was later further developed by Einstein and a physicist named Nathan Rosen.

Einstein and Rosen concluded that there might be bridges between points in space-time—shortcuts for long journeys across the universe, reducing both distance and time taken. This has the additional benefit of reducing time-dilation effects associated with extreme velocity. In regular space travel at high speeds, time passes much slower for passengers on a rapidly accelerating starship than people on a planet.[6]

This strange theoretical object came to be known as an Einstein-Rosen bridge but is more popularly known as a *wormhole*. It is necessary for us to accept that Einstein's theory of general relativity mathematically predicts the existence of wormholes. Thankfully, we don't need to read all the complicated equations for ourselves!

Though no wormhole is currently known by astronomers, it is understood that the entrances would likely be spherical, with a stretched tunnel between them that could be either straight or twisted like a writhing snake. Naturally occurring wormholes would probably be both infinitesimally small and incredibly unstable. Any wormhole useful to space travel would almost certainly need to be artificially created by incredibly advanced technology.

Theoretical physics research suggests that a wormhole containing "exotic matter" could stay open and unchanging for lengthy periods.[7] Exotic matter includes negative energy density and tremendous negative pressure, but this type of material has been only indirectly detected in the behavior of certain vacuum states as part of quantum field theory. Yet, it may be within the capabilities of some alien races to produce quantities of exotic matter for this purpose.

It was long believed that natural singularities such as black holes would be impossible to traverse in a craft. The incredible gravitational pressures would stretch and squeeze the vehicle before eventually obliterating it for good. Gaurav Khanna, professor of physics at the University of Massachusetts, has led a team in researching whether some black holes might be different from others. They deduced that if a black hole is massive and rotating, the singularity might be quite gentle and permit a ship to pass through.

Khanna's colleague Caroline Mallary designed a computational model to assess the effects on a craft entering a very large rotating singularity, akin to Sagittarius A, which lies at the center of our own galaxy. Mallary concludes that spacecraft might experience little or no strong adverse effects as it entered a massive singularity, opening the possibility of using such black holes as intergalactic portals for travel. Where the spaceship would end up is, of course, not at all clear, but it may be that other advanced civilizations have unlocked the secrets of such travel.[8]

When we are ready to try this possible method of travel, one of the safest options may be the supermassive black hole at the center of our galaxy, and it might just be our ticket out of the Milky Way and into a different galaxy.

Though we can't hope for written witness accounts from people present on Earth at the time the mothership arrived, there are oral histories and reports of more recent visitations to Earth by beings allegedly arriving from the Pleiades. These ancient legends occur in various cultures all around the globe. Here's a quick look at a few examples.

Wilfred Buck, a science educator of the Opaskwayak Cree Nation, explains that his tribal group see a great trickster in the sky when they look up at Orion. This stellar being is pointing toward the Pleiades. The Cree Indians claim that where the Pleiades is positioned, there exists a hole in the sky—our planet's connection to the cosmos. It is Buck's opinion that this story refers to an example of the spatial anomaly modern science knows as a wormhole.

In Buck's telling of ancient lore, humans were lowered down from the hole in the sky on a single thread created by Mother Spider. "We originate from the stars. We are star people," Buck says, adding, "The genesis mythologies say this is where we come from. We come from those stars, we are related to those stars. Once we finish doing what we come here to do, we go back up to those stars."[9]

The Cree are indeed not the only indigenous population that claim an ancestral link to the Pleiades. The same theme is found among cultures spread across the Americas, including the Hopi, Dakota, and Maya. Elsewhere we see the same claims among the Balinese and the Tana Toraja (in Indonesia), the Japanese, and the Taiwanese.

All the Australian Aboriginal nations have dreaming lore about the Pleiades. Many of them tell of a human origination story associated with these stars and seven sisters who came from them to Earth. It is worth pointing out that Australian Aboriginals are the holders of the world's oldest recognized culture and the most deeply rooted oral history. We really do not know just how old some of the Aboriginal dreaming stories are; some literally go back tens of thousands of years.

One other connection to this story appears in the fascinating book series written by British researcher Leonard Farra. We have had a personal relationship with Leonard for a little while now, and he has supplied articles for one of our websites and sent us copies of two of his books. Farra has written a three-book series on his investigation into links between various ancient cultures and the Pleiades. What is perhaps less known to some of those familiar with his work is that this project was initially inspired by an experience that occurred while he was attending the mediumship circle of the noted British psychic medium Gerry Sherrick.

You may know Gerry Sherrick as one of the supernatural experts involved with the Enfield poltergeist case, a story more recently featured in the plot of a Hollywood blockbuster.

The sessions with Sherrick are described in some detail in Leonard's first book, *Genesis Seven*. He recounts the channeling of a long-dead Mexican village elder. This spirit told the group, through Sherrick, that he had lived at a time when seven saucer-like craft landed near his village, many centuries ago. The human-like alien beings that emerged were tall, light-skinned, telepathic, and equipped with many advanced technologies. The leader of the visitors informed him that they had arrived from the Pleiades, but it was then clarified that they came from "beyond the time barrier."

The star people told the local Mexican leader that he would be given a device capable of contacting them. They also informed this person that the seed of the travelers was to be sown in the wombs of the local people's daughters "in order that great leaders would be born" and that this would advance humanity from its present state. The visitors warned the human elder that his people would give birth to children that wouldn't look like members of their tribe and these children would be "high in stature."[10]

You can easily find out more about Leonard Farra's globetrotting investigations in his books *The Pleiades Legacy: The Stone Age—The Return of the Gods*, *The Pleiades Legacy: The Old World*, and *The Pleiades Legacy: The New World*. The information explored here appears in his (now out of print) book *Genesis Seven*. Leonard was so impacted by those first experiences with mediumship that he set out on a lifelong quest for evidence of these purported alien visitations in the ancient past.

When we received a copy of *Genesis Seven*, we must admit to being left somewhat shocked. There are astonishing overlaps between the information recorded during the Sherrick channeling sessions and things Daniella encountered during her personal time slips.

Sherrick had retrieved details of the arrival of the Pleiadian time travelers and their insemination of local women. Daniella had witnessed the aftermath with giant-sized Pleiadian-human hybrids leading the local people. It is hard not to see this as the workings of some higher intelligence, skillfully popping puzzle pieces into place all around us.

Such matters as these are not the sort of things we can call mere coincidence. There is the apparent intelligent ordering of events and arranging of the essential connections. Somebody or something is apparently helping us to put all this bizarre evidence together. We have to say that it comes as no surprise at all to us that entities associated with the Pleiades had control of a wormhole-like spatial anomaly, allowing them instantaneous voyages and time travel. On many occasions during Daniella's shamanic journeys, or time slips, she was given the understanding that the aliens were not only space travelers but time travelers. The fact that Sherrick is told these humanoids came from "beyond the time barrier" makes perfect sense in that context.

If you know even a little about the ancient Mayan culture, you will be aware that they had a bizarre preoccupation with recording and calculating vast spans of time.

The Maya not only used several different calendar systems, but these were also used interchangeably to track many different cyclical periods. The famous Long Count calendar follows a cycle of one baktun, or 5,125 years. It has been noted that five baktuns cover 25,630 years, incredibly close to a complete astronomical precession cycle of approximately 26,000 years. This may seem quite an extraordinary interest for an ancient culture, but when you look closer at some of the units of time used by the Maya, things get a whole lot stranger.

Keep in mind that the Mayan culture itself lasted for perhaps two millennia or so, yet they used measurements such as the kalabtun of 157,704 years; the k'inchiltun of 3,154,071 years; and the alautun, an incredible 63,081,429-year-long period.

Doesn't it seem just a little bit weird that the low-tech early post-Neolithic Maya people needed to discuss such a vast period of time, one that happens to begin when our first primate ancestors inherited the earth from the recently removed dinosaurs?

It is not just that there seem to be strange measurement periods but that in many cases dates engraved on monuments are celebrating events in the distant future, things that won't happen until several thousand more years have passed. As you zoom in a bit on the ancient Maya, it becomes possible to detect the fingerprints of time-traveling beings alongside the normal workings of a megalithic human society.

Even the other periods highlighted above have peculiar correspondences: a kalabtun covers the period when modern humans emerged from archaic *Homo sapiens*, whereas a k'inchiltun takes us to the start of the genus *Homo*. Properly exploring this subject and adequately assessing Daniella's personal experiences with the ancient Mayan culture would require a separate book, but we have comfortably established links between the indigenous people of the Americas, the Pleiades, and wormholes. Stories around the world claim much the same things.

Aboriginal Australians from across their continent have ancient stories about seven sisters from the Pleiades that once visited Earth. Additionally, these ladies are often pursued by a hunter associated with Orion. Instead of spiderwebs and cosmic threads coming down to our world, Aboriginal lore speaks of these beings moving through magical tunnels, climbing rapidly expanding tree trunks, or making use of giant ropes.[11] All these methods for returning to outer space have an uncanny resemblance to what scientists describe as wormholes.

The bottom line is that there is the possibility within known physics that highly technologically advanced aliens might create a wormhole and travel to Earth from a distant star. It is therefore astonishing that ancient cultures describe visitors from space arriving from beyond the time barrier via tunnels, serpent ropes, magical tree trunks, and other methods that all sound like laypersons' descriptions of just such rifts torn in the fabric of space-time.

CHAPTER 10

THE SENTIENT MOTHERSHIP AND HER TEARS OF GLASS

Uploading allows a creature near immortality, enables reboots, and allows it to survive under a variety of conditions that carbon-based life forms cannot. In addition, silicon appears to be a better medium for information processing than the brain itself.

—SUSAN SCHNEIDER, professor of
philosophy and cognitive science

As we have seen, there is compelling scientific evidence that indicates life was seeded on Earth. Support has been offered for the validity of people witnessing wormholes ripped open in the skies above them. We have already encountered potential extraterrestrial technologies, investigated psychical communications, and even traveled through space and time. Despite all this persuasive information, we have not yet explored the most compelling scientific proofs for Alcheringa's astonishing visitation story.

We understand that any contact event involving extraordinarily advanced extraterrestrial intelligence would be multifaceted and inherently complex in nature. That has required an astonishing collection of subjects to be brought together. With the foundation in place, we can finally explore the "smoking gun" evidence that I am sure you have been looking forward to. We need to approach the big question: Did a vast sentient crystalline mothership really arrive here hundreds of thousands of years ago, only to be destroyed in orbit?

The mothership is described as enormous, with a crew count of about fifty thousand beings. This was not a metal craft like the human engineered shuttles and rockets. Alcheringa explains that it was rather like a vast saucer, grown from a crystalline material. Further, it is revealed that the ship was itself alive, having a self-aware consciousness imbued throughout the structure.

Humanity is at the beginning of a revolution in material engineering. In the future, we will move beyond even 3D printing and smart materials to self-replicating nanobot swarms and programmable matter. These predictions are based on the potentials of known science and the current direction of engineering research.

The description of a starship that is not built but instead grown from within a crystalline matrix may appear to be utterly unthinkable. However, this is absolutely in line with expectations researchers have regarding the future of programmable matter. Objects in the future may be able to change shape, alter their utility, and even "learn" from interactions with their users. Swarms of nanobots could take forms as required, becoming a car and then dissipating to become invisible clouds. Twenty-five years ago, when Alcheringa spoke to Valerie Barrow, nobody would have known that self-constructing craft was a future technology.

The mention of crystal as the key material for the ship is compelling. Silicon crystal, such as quartz, is well understood to have essential qualities for advanced information technologies. Silicon readily allows for storage and processing of data when integrated into computer systems. The crystalline structure of the craft likely enabled the uploading of an advanced artificial intelligence to inhabit the super-structure of the vessel. This would make a great deal of sense. Rather than limiting yourself to an onboard computer system, the entire enormous ship is the computer, allowing for astonishing processing capabilities.

We have repeatedly heard leading scientists predicting advanced extraterrestrial beings will use silica networks to house superintelligence, so the signature of this technology is something we should expect to see if aliens arrived on Earth.

There seems to be an overlap between Alcheringa's mothership and a description in the ancient Hebrew religious text known as the Book of Enoch. Tradition ascribes the Book of Enoch to the great-grandfather of Noah. You might have already heard ancient astronaut theorists claim that Enoch's writings describe interactions with visiting star beings during a period before the biblical flood. We can't prove that Enoch met extraterrestrials, but I think the following highlighted section certainly sounds strangely related to the description of the crystalline mothership:

> *They elevated me aloft to heaven. I proceeded until I arrived at a wall built with stones of crystal. A vibrating flame surrounded it, which began to strike me with terror. Into this vibrating flame I entered; And drew nigh to a spacious habitation built also with stones of crystal. Its walls too, as well as pavement, were formed with stones of crystal, and crystal likewise was the ground. Its roof had the appearance of agitated stars and flashes of lightning; and among them were cherubim of fire in a stormy sky. A flame burned around its walls; and its*

*portal blazed with fire. When I entered into this dwell-
ing, it was hot as fire and cold as ice. No trace of delight
or of life was there. Terror overwhelmed me, and a fear-
ful shaking seized me.*[1]

The description offered by Enoch sounds very much as if
he was carried up into a sizable crystalline vessel, a craft surrounded by powerful energy shields. What are the chances
that this obscure text would refer to something sounding so
like the details of the already-mentioned alien technologies?

Another related account from more recent times comes
from the legendary encounter between US military personnel and a mysterious phenomenon in Rendlesham Forest
(UK). For several days, a wide range of objects was observed
by dozens of officers in the close vicinity of USAF Wood-
bridge. The base secretly protected nuclear weapons. Initially, several glowing orbs of blue, red, orange, and white
were observed by soldiers. One glowing red orb hovered
twenty feet above the ground before exploding and being
replaced by a structured craft (making me think we really
need to think again about the nature of "ball lightning").

One evening a triangular craft was encountered in the
forest. Jim Penniston approached to examine it closer and
discovered that it was engraved with hieroglyphic-like
markings. Penniston recalls, "I noticed the fabric of the shell
was more like a smooth, opaque, black glass."[2]

In *ALCHERINGA . . . When the First Ancestors Were Created*, Valerie offers the understanding that after the mothership was destroyed in orbit the main body of the ship fell
to Earth: "'Are you aware if pieces of the mothership came
to Earth?' 'It sort of melted. There were pieces all around.'"[3]

Valerie suggests that the craft fell to Earth and became
moldavite.[4] There is no doubt that moldavite, a translucent
green tektite glass, is a unique material. It is also undoubtedly

the result of a massive object falling from space, impacting in Bavaria, Germany.[5] Moldavite has long been considered a powerful tool for spiritual awakening and is even connected with the legends of the holy grail. I will leave it to readers to decide where this material fits into this story. I encourage you to acquire a piece for yourself and see if it affects you as many people have claimed. It certainly makes lovely jewelry.

Our investigation started by considering the possibility that moldavite might be the central part of the mothership. Eventually, we were forced to reject this, as every type of geological dating used puts moldavite formation at about 14.7 million years ago, as the result of an impact that caused the Nördlinger Ries crater. Details on Valerie's website suggest that the events occurred "700,000 years ago in 4th-dimensional time . . . [and] 900,000 years in 3rd-dimensional time."[6]

We considered that perhaps an anomalous date might be produced from an examination of material associated with a time-traveling extraterrestrial spaceship. And though that is an intriguing thought, the melted rock at the crater site is also dated to the same extremely early period. That does not preclude moldavite from being debris from an extraterrestrial craft, but I had to conclude that it was at least not the one we were looking for at this time.

We were still looking for anomalous melted crystalline debris. Moldavite had been discounted, but tektite still represented precisely the type of stuff we should be looking into. Tektites are rare geological artifacts, always high in silica, and most often associated with extraterrestrial impact events. The material is produced by extreme heat during high-energy events. We seemed to be on the right trail with tektite research. Alcheringa had revealed that after a traitor lowered the protective field, the ship was hit by electromagnetic entrainment weaponry that shat-tered and super-heated the hull. The craft did not merely explode but came apart and melted. The resulting molten crystalline material then fell to Earth. Being silica glass, it could potentially survive for millions of years.

Valerie's book not only provided a good idea of what kind of material I needed to look for but also indicated a target geographical region for us to focus our search. The story of the attack includes many smaller saucers fleeing from the enemy attack. Most were destroyed before they got far, and others were pursued as they attempted to get to the surface. This is the experience I had in my past life shamanic journey: being one of the pilots under pursuit heading toward the ground.

The few survivors are described as crashing or landing in Southeast Australia. You will recall that the landing site was near Gosford, about one hour north of Sydney. This is important because, assuming craft are trying to flee almost straight down, this gives us an indication of the mothership's orbital location. Being able to close in on a reduced target area for the debris field was massively important, as this saved scouring the entire planet for evidence. Still, a part of me thought I was on a mission impossible with this search—that there was no way I was going to find the wreckage of an alien craft, especially one that was blown to bits in outer space hundreds of thousands of years ago. That was, of course, only until I found it!

From Antarctica, through Southeast Australia, and onward to the northwest lies the Australasian tektite strewn field that finally comes to an end in South China.[7] Strewn fields are geographical clusters of tektites, all originating from a shared causal event.

As mentioned previously, moldavite is the best-known class of tektite glass. Tektite glass does not form every time our planet is impacted. In fact, there are only four identified tektite strewn fields despite the many cosmic impact events during geological history. In order of age, the tektite strewn fields are North American (34 million years), Central European (14 million years), Ivory Coast (1 million years), and Australasian (0.78 million years).[8]

The first three of these strewn fields are associated with identified impact craters, each of considerable size. The oldest of these, the North American strewn field, is linked to the Chesapeake Bay impact crater, which is more than twenty-five miles in diameter. There is something extraordinary about the fact that only four of these strewn fields exist despite large numbers of asteroids and comets impacting our planet. This immediately makes all of them a little bit strange and anomalous.

The oddity of the tektite subject grows far more significant once you investigate the youngest of these strewn fields. Australasian tektites are known as australites, and they really are in a division of their own. The first significant fact about australite is that, despite being produced recently (in geological terms) and being exceptionally widely dispersed (associated microtektites reached more than 10 percent of the earth's surface), there is no associated crater.[9]

This is bizarre, as there should logically be a crater far more sizable than the one known to be at the Chesapeake Bay. The hole left behind would also be considerably younger than all the others and therefore would be more obvious. Scientists suggest the object responsible for all this material (assuming a compact solid sphere) would have been around 0.6–1.5 miles in diameter. If such an asteroid hit the planet hard enough to cover 10 percent of the globe with debris, it is projected the crater would be about 12.5 miles wide. So why are there no surface signs of this massive object touching down? The distribution of australite and the lack of source impact site have indeed caused a great deal of head-scratching among geologists.

A second conundrum has prompted far more heated debate over the last century: the specific mechanism of australite formation and shaping. Tektites are composed of a rapidly heated material thrown through the air. Initially, tektites are formed from liquid glass. The glass starts to cool during flight, and while partially fluidic, the material takes on specific aerodynamic shapes. The pieces are generally hard by the time they land on the ground, but this leaves a problem in the case of australites.

Australite has an additional form not known among other tektites: the *flanged button*, which involved a unique double melting process. We need to explore this characteristic in a bit more detail. The look of these australite buttons just screams "We are from space" when you examine them. They look somewhat like small flying saucers. NASA scientists analyzed australite fragments as a part of their Apollo program's craft design programs, realizing the glassy objects offered a unique understanding of the shapes that best suit entering our atmosphere.

One NASA report says this about the nature of the fragments:

> *Experiment and analysis indicate that the button-type australites were derived from glassy spheres which entered or re-entered the atmosphere as cold solid bodies; in case of average-size specimens, the entry direction was nearly horizontal and the entry speed between 6.5 and 11.2 km/sec. Terrestrial origin of such spheres is impossible because of extremely high deceleration rates at low altitudes.[10]*

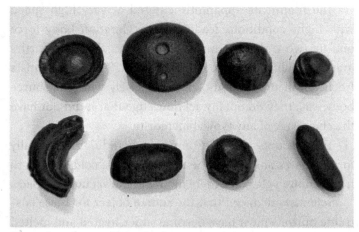

Examples of australites, also known as tektites

Australite sample one

Australite sample two

The fragments apparently entered at very high speed with flight conditions leading to deceleration body force one or two orders of magnitude higher than the earth's gravitational force at the time of impact. Though scientists freely admit that nobody knows precisely what the source body was, they do openly acknowledge that it did not have the chemistry of any typical meteorite.

There is only one environment where liquids naturally form spheres and where the temperature is cold enough to freeze molten glass in a mere moment: the vacuum of space.

Scientists deduced that the source object for these australite buttons must have become super-heated and melted to a liquid just prior to the near-instantaneous cooling of the glassy spheres. These glass spheres then rained down through the earth's atmosphere and began to heat up again, partially melting and then allowing unique button shapes to be sculpted by the atmospheric resistance.

Researchers of this subject have suggested all kinds of solutions for the source of australites, ranging from a chunk of material blown off the moon or Mars hitting our atmosphere, right through to an asteroid impacting in Southeast Asia and throwing material sixty miles back up into space before it rained down again. Every scenario suggested over the last century of investigation has eventually ended without a convincing conclusion; none explained all the associated anomalies. Liquified rock cools as it moves through the air, and as such even if some had enough energy to reach space (which is unlikely) it would solidify during the journey.[11]

The single fact agreed upon by all involved in australite research is that the chain of events that created australite buttons was unique in 4.5 billion years. The widely accepted dating for this material's formation lies between 770,000 to

790,000 years ago. Such a unique finding is a glaring scientific anomaly.[12]

The composition of individual australite fragments ranges, but they are often up to 80 percent silica derived from melted quartz crystal. This is astonishing, as quartz crystal would never naturally compose the bulk of an asteroid, comet, or meteorite. From what I was able to find, it seems that silica is distributed in space, but quartz crystals rarely form beyond planetary environments. For the sake of useful comparison, our own planet's crust contains approximately 12 percent silica crystal. Surely, then, a lump of quartz crystal about one-half mile in diameter is mind-bogglingly unlikely.[13]

Australites also contain significant percentages of aluminum combined with about twenty-three additional elements. I am not a chemist or a geologist, but relevant papers mention that specific percentages of component chemicals make it unlike known meteoric material. They also exhibit an abnormal nickel-chromium balance, and some smaller samples contain magnesium-26 in excess of 20 percent (unlike Earth rocks).[14]

Experiments involving the simulating of molten glass ejected into the atmosphere do not produce results resembling the australite primary shapes. These experiments revealed that the spheroidal forms of australites formed in an environment with far lower atmospheric density than the earth's surface. These results stand in direct opposition to any hypothesis involving australites originating from the earth or any atmosphere-blanketed planet.[15]

NASA research on the entrance trajectory of australites precludes any object coming from outside the solar system. As a period of slowly increasing heating is needed to explain the liquefaction of the tektite source material, it was determined the objects traveled along orbits almost parallel to the surface of the earth. The logical deduction indicated the decaying orbit of a "natural" satellite.[16]

The most massive pieces of Southeast Asian tektites, known as Muong Nong layered tektites, weigh more than forty-four pounds. These large pieces of material are made up of multiple layers of glass that was once molten. There is no well-accepted explanation for this strange layering.

With the incredible weight of some of the Muong Nong tektites, it is evident that they could not have flown far from an impact site. They are just too heavy, yet there is no sign of a crater in the local region. The evidence observed seems to fit well with material falling from the sky rather than being displaced by a local impact.[17]

Norm Lehrman is recognized as an authority on australites. Not only has he investigated them extensively for many years but he is also an exploration geologist. Lehrman has quite conclusively revealed that no object impacted the earth to form the australites. Instead, the evidence points to a swarm involving dozens of chunks from a larger parent body breaking apart.

Over several hours, these structurally weak bolides, moving through the atmosphere, exploded, causing immensely powerful aerial bursts. Lehrman doubts any of these larger pieces reached the ground level to cause cratering. This meshes well with observations by australite hunters that they are found in concentration within small distantly spaced locations, and with none in between. Where each bolide broke apart, it showered the ground below in localized fashion.

Lehrman's final proof of theory was his discovery of a Muong Nong–type australite piece that had another small fragment welded to the top. The material exhibited signs of cooling for some period before a second molten layer arrived. The stone provided direct and unequivocal signs of a second airburst event no less than ten minutes later but perhaps a few hours later. This profile fits with fragments from a single disintegrating body following a single trajectory in sequence.[18]

This means we had a half-mile-wide body made almost entirely from quartz crystal in orbit around the planet 780,000 years ago. I calculate the orbital position as being between the Antarctic and southern Australia. This peculiar body then exploded into pieces, with much of it transformed into liquid glass. The glass instantly cooled into spherules.

As larger chunks of debris and smaller australite spheres moved into a decaying orbit, they heated. The smaller spheres began to melt and became oblate, exhibiting secondary melting before impact. These rained down almost directly below the point of initial explosion, arriving in southern Australia.

Larger pieces of the parent body had not been liquified and transformed into glass. These pieces formed the bolide swarm and, as they broke up, the many other shapes of tektite, such as teardrops and dumbbells, exhibiting only a single period of melting. Those chunks that came closest to ground level before exploding gave rise to the strange Muong Nong layered tektite material in Southeast Asia.

Comets do not slowly orbit our planet, asteroids have a low silica composition, quartz does not form in the vacuum of space, and lunar rock simply does not fit the bill. What, then, was this huge parent body that exploded and gave rise to these unique australite buttons?

We have here what we would have to call a hand-in-glove fit between Alcheringa's download and the observed scientific evidence. This astronomical and geological anomaly remains unexplained until we factor in a large quartz-crystal artificially intelligent extraterrestrial craft, initially orbiting the earth and then fired upon and destroyed by enemy forces. With the destruction of the ship, survivors sped down to the ground almost directly below, landing in southern Australia. The initial wave of debris followed behind them, accelerated downward by the initial explosion.

It is interesting to note that in historical times Aboriginal people considered australite buttons to be powerful sacred artifacts. Some of their lore suggests that when a clever man is given his power by the spirits, they replace his internal organs with crystals and australites.

I must admit to feeling slightly sad writing this account. Tens of thousands of souls perished as the explosion shattered the colony ship. These were also the last moments of existence for the self-aware intelligence inhabiting the crystal ship itself. The mothership was a living being beyond our comprehension, experiencing her death high above an alien world. Alcheringa tells us that the ship's name was Rexegena. Does a self-aware artificial intelligence feel pain? Did she cry? I must wonder if it is merely a coincidence that today the similar-sounding word *exogenesis* refers to life coming to Earth from space.

In a peculiar twist to this story, there is some reason to suspect that fragments of the craft eventually ended up in one of the most important holy sites on our planet: Mecca. The most sacred place in the Islamic faith is the Kaaba at Mecca, and cemented into the eastern corner are seven or eight pieces of black stone. The surrounding silver casing strongly resembles a sacred *yoni* (vulva). It is known that these relics were already considered holy in pre-Islamic times. Correctly known as the Hajar al-Aswad (stone from paradise), the fragments of material included in the Kaaba have long been suspected to be tektites. Sadly, direct examination by scientists is not in the cards.

The mythology of the black stone is a genesis story, which explains why they are in the eastern corner—this being the direction of the rising sun and therefore symbolic of birth. The pilgrim circles the Kaaba seven times, the number of readily visible stars in the Pleiades cluster. It is claimed that the stone was brought down to Earth by angels involved in the creation of the first humans, Adam and Eve. The material is said to have initially been pure white, only turning black after absorbing sins. The mothership was purportedly white before the explosion.

Perhaps most intriguing of all is another telling of the mythology in which the black stone was once an angel placed in the Garden of Eden to watch over Adam. This reminds me once again of the black monolith standing amid the first humans in *2001: A Space Odyssey*. The angel was punished for failing in its task by being transformed into a black jewel. God then gave the black stone the power of speech.[19]

Is it purely a coincidence that in Islamic tradition a strange black silicate material with cosmic origins has intelligence, can communicate, and is connected to human origins? Did an intelligence from within the stone tell someone this story?

CHAPTER 11

METEORIC BOMBARDMENT, POLE SHIFT, AND CLIMATE CHAOS

> *Surprisingly our age estimates prove that they originated 777,000 years ago with a deviation of 16,000 years. Within the error margin, this matches the age of the Australasian tektites.*
>
> —WINFRIED SCHWARZ, PhD, geochronologist

Alcheringa claimed that news of the intended betrayal of the colony mission reached the leaders of the allied council even before the craft had been destroyed. It was, however, too late to prevent the attack.

A short time later a squadron of alliance ships left for Earth, this time a fleet of military craft. These vessels arrived in orbit around Earth five years after the ambush. While they did contact the few survivors and offer retrieval, this was not their primary mission. It had been decided that, as the forces occupying Earth had broken their treaty agreement with the council and destroyed a peaceful mission, there should be appropriate consequences.

These "space police" were described as members of the leonine race, a militarized society of feline humanoids. This species is described as having a long history of combat with the more hostile alien races. Although the ships had advanced onboard weapons, they utilized meteors as their main surface-to-ground artillery.

Large asteroids could be located and then dragged through space using a type of tractor beam technology (gravity distortion?) and then launched at specific regions on a planet's surface. This type of planetary bombardment caused immense devastation; a planet could even be neutralized with an extinction level event. As Valerie Barrow writes in *ALCHERINGA . . . When the First Ancestors Were Created*, "We can pull down a meteor and direct it, some are so big they will shatter a planet. We don't just create tidal waves."[1]

The military force sent a team to the ground and entered the underground bases of the enemy, warning them to return technologies captured from the colony mission. The hostile forces were then to evacuate the planet as initially agreed in their treaty. Many of these beings fled through a wormhole back to their home system in Orion, and others refused to comply.

The enforcers engaged the enemy after the failed negotiations and began a bombardment from space involving several large asteroids. Even being underground was not enough to entirely evade the aftermath of such an attack.

These descriptions perhaps sound incredible, bizarre aliens battling in space above this world and even under its surface. Some aspects of this are impossible to prove without locating the subterranean facilities, but there couldn't have been such a cosmic conflagration without leaving some trace.

The effect of even a single reasonably sized meteor smashing into our planet would leave evidence. What, then, of multiple hits from all directions?

It seemed likely that such a significant and highly anomalous bombardment event should be well known to scientists. This multidirectional rain of death would initiate massive effects on the planet's environment for a long time afterward, leaving craters scarring the surface.

We were surprised that we had never heard of anything like that happening after the volatile early period following Earth's formation billions of years ago. We felt that perhaps there was just no evidence available or it would be well known. Something told us not to give up on validating the impact claims. If we found signs of a global impact-induced cataclysm about 780,000 years ago, it would provide us with a very well evidenced narrative. The ship had been located and the debris dated. If one more event relevant to Alcheringa's story could be identified and linked to the same date, we would be in a solid position.

It took a while to track down, but I eventually discovered there really had been a bombardment of Earth by multiple asteroids. The dates for the impacts were posited to be somewhere between 770,000 to 790,000 years ago. The reason this was not well known was that the discovery had only just been announced in late 2016 as a brief news item.

The discovery had been made during a geological study by a team from Heidelberg University. Samples from sites in Asia, Australia, Canada, Central America, and Tasmania all pointed to a convergent impact event. The team's models predicted that there would have been massive earthquakes, powerful tsunamis, and widespread fires. The chemical analysis indicated that this event involved chemically distinct asteroids rather than fragments of a single body, asteroids that hit the planet from several directions at the same time. Beyond the immediate destruction caused, dust and gases would have been thrown up into the atmosphere, blocking sunlight and lowering temperatures. This was a major planetary cataclysm.[2]

There is an interesting article published on Graham Hancock's website written by a Croatian-Italian engineer, Flavio Barbiero. His research suggested that if a large enough object impacted Earth at the right speed and angle, it might slightly change the rotation of the planet.[3]

This rotational modification would initiate an axial pole shift or Earth crust displacement. Barbiero spent most of his professional life working on research projects for the Italian navy as a specialist in gyroscopic motion, retiring at the rank of admiral. He suspected that such an axial shift event may even have previously moved Antarctica to its present-day location and left a once-pleasant land under thick ice. Legendary scientist Albert Einstein famously gave his support to the scientific possibility of this type of planetary shift.

There is substantial evidence that suggests an axial pole shift event occurred on Venus in the remote past. Venus is the only planet in our solar system spinning both clockwise and entirely opposite to its path around the sun.[4] This is profoundly strange.

Astronomers have noticed that Venus's rotation is rapidly slowing. Considering that Venus already has the slowest rotation of any planetary body in the solar system, there is no logic behind this rapid decrease in speed.[5] It looks very much like Venus's crust was once turned right over and that it is now in the process of correcting its direction of rotation. If this could happen on Venus, we must take seriously the possibility that it can occur on Earth.

Could the multidirectional meteoric bombardment 780,000 years ago unleash the horror of an axial pole shift?

Apart from the German geological research that suggested a global cataclysm ensued, it is notable that close to eight hundred thousand years ago, a shift occurred in the dominant periodicity of glacial oscillations. These changes between cold and warm periods went from a forty-one-thousand-year duration to a one-hundred-thousand-year-long period. This is known as the Mid-Pleistocene Transition, and to this day nobody understands why it happened. This was a profound and mysterious shift in the well-established climate cycles of our planet.

The Mid-Pleistocene Transition may have a different cause. The exact date remains unclear. However, it makes you suspect that something fundamental changed in respect to the planet's rotation, tilt, and journey around the sun. Paleoclimate models also reveal that, from after eight hundred thousand years ago, the global climate generally became far less predictable, heading into chaotic wild fluctuations not previously observed.[6]

Moving away from my personal speculation and back to scientific fact, another enormous change occurred 780,000 years ago. This is precisely the timing for the planet's last total magnetic pole shift. There is some reason to suspect that this reversal was related to the other events underway.

Consider here that during the previous twenty million years magnetic pole reversals held a pattern of one occurrence every two hundred thousand to three hundred thousand years. The apparent oddity here is that this cycle became disrupted 780,000 years ago, and we are now hundreds of thousands of years overdue for another reversal.

The earth's magnetic field plays a crucial role in protecting the planet from solar and cosmic rays. When the poles switch, this protective shield diminishes to as little as one-tenth of its usual strength. Geophysicists tend to think that the reversal process takes centuries, during which time radiation would be able to penetrate closer to the ground. Eventually, this radiation could reach the surface of the earth, rendering some regions uninhabitable and potentially causing localized mutagenic extinction events for some organisms.[7]

There is a well-understood relationship between the magnetic fields of our planet and the fields of the sun. These cosmic fields interact and provoke corresponding changes. It is considered possible that the magnetic reversals on our world are at least partly triggered by changes in the electromagnetic fields of the sun. Perhaps the disruption of Earth's field was induced by something unusual about solar dynamics?

Today we are at the beginning of a magnetic reversal. The poles are wandering incredibly fast, and the field strength is rapidly decreasing. Geoscientists are expressing considerable concern about the possibility of an imminent total reversal.[8] This would have profound implications for us as a technological civilization, as there would be electromagnetic consequences. We might see the disabling of satellites and dire effects on the electrical grid. Energy from the sun can potentially enter the grid and cause the collapse of the global power system.

The peculiar thing is that we are currently witnessing abnormal solar behavior. Solar physicists are now saying there are never observed types of activity in the energy dynamics of our nearby star. The number of sunspots has dropped incredibly, even during peaks of the cycle, and this type of drop is linked to sudden violent outbursts. The transition period from Solar Cycle 23 to Solar Cycle 24 was the deepest in more than a century, with 817 spotless days. The previous switchover evidenced only 309 clear days.

The year 2018 had about 210 days without any sunspots. Solar Cycle 24 has been lacking notably large sunspots. Suffice it to say that any powerful solar storms thrown our way while overall activity is low are bad news. Overall reductions in solar activity can also potentially usher in short-duration "mini" ice ages.

It is difficult to establish whether the magnetic reversal 780,000 years ago was directly harmful to early humans. We have already discovered that humans are sensitive to the field changes at a subconscious level. Perhaps the change in magnetic fields powerfully impacts human consciousness?

It is very intriguing that Alcheringa mentions that the star people were suffering a great deal from solar radiation problems on the planet surface. This is most likely just due to their biological and anatomical makeup, but it might also have been connected to unusually powerful solar activity.

So many powerful and anomalous events overlapping in time takes us far beyond the limits of coincidence. We have enigmas piled on anomalies, embedded in a period of previously unexplained events centered on 780,000 years ago.

Any scientist who argues there is nothing to see here has switched their brain to a low power setting. There will of course always be those "skeptics" who dismiss everything that does not fit the consensus narrative or threatens the existing paradigm. Like it or not, we are looking at scientific facts that don't fit with the mainstream account of prehistory.

We could leave this investigation here and be left with a profoundly changed understanding of the remote past and the foundations of the human story. This is, of course, not the end of our investigation. It's time to take a much closer look at the emergence of our own human species, *Homo sapiens.*

CHAPTER 12

OUR FIRST ANCESTORS WERE *HOMO PLEIADIAN*

The way to evolve a human from a chimp-human ancestor is not to speed the ticking of the molecular clock as a whole. Rather the secret is to have rapid change occur in sites where those changes make an important difference in an organism's functioning.

—KATHERINE POLLARD, biostatistician

Could visiting extraterrestrials have left us something equivalent to a genetic message in a bottle?

Professor Davies at the SETI Post-Detection Taskgroup has admitted to a personal attraction to the idea extraterrestrials might have encoded a "we were here" signature in our DNA. Davies considers this an intriguing but remote possibility that's well worth exploring. I consider such a genomic alien signature to be a demonstrable fact.

You might assume that leading figures in astrophysics, astrobiology, and astronomy would be the ones to find such an extraterrestrial genetic signature. How could such evidence be missed by academics and left for discovery by me, a mere information technology professional, even if one fanatically researching evolutionary biology and ancient mysteries?

The crucial differences between the relevant academics and me are threefold. First, I have had external assistance from parties with inside knowledge. Second, I am actively looking for anomalies in the genetic data. Finally, I am a highly intuitive Asperger-type person. This last point may seem a little bit peculiar, but it is incredibly relevant.

Neuropsychologists Gabriel de la Torre and Manuel García from the University of Cádiz in Spain published a fascinating paper in the journal *Acta Astronautica*. Their research argues that the preoccupation with extraterrestrial radio signals might be a complete distraction from the more likely phenomena associated with advanced alien life. The University of Cádiz team suggests that rather than radio signals, an alien intelligence might be manifesting itself in dimensions that usually escape our perception, maybe as quantum phenomena, higher dimensional physics, or even dark energy. This echoes the opinions of some academics that suggest extraordinarily advanced aliens may also manifest as the laws of physics.

The two psychologists ran a series of experiments to better understand how perception is limited by personal cognition and expectations. The findings from the trials offered a startling result: half of the 137 participants were unable to notice an erroneous inclusion in an image of a barren planetary landscape. Even more alarming was that those persons who fared the worst were those with a tendency toward logical, right-brained thinking, which is common among academics. De la Torre explained:

> *In addition, our surprise was greater, since before doing the test to see the inattentional blindness, we assessed the participants with a series of questions to determine their cognitive style—whether they were more intuitive or rational—and it turned out that the*

intuitive individuals identified the gorilla in our photo more often than those more rational and methodical subjects.[1]

In short summary, a team of right-brained scientists is the least likely group to spot a glaring anomaly in the data. It should be expected that a left-brained outsider, busy reviewing the same material, is more likely to notice something unusual. As we already heard from Davies, his opinion is that a discovery is most likely to come from someone outside the SETI community. He expects that the person will discover a persistent data anomaly "and other people will dismiss it until it forces itself on the community."[2]

The signature for genetic engineering of our hominin ancestors is a complex subject. This is because there is not one single change that was carried out but quite a considerable number of modifications to different parts of the genome.

If an advanced alien race visited Earth in remote prehistory and decided to modify an organism—let's specifically suggest a hominin ancestor of ours—it might be hard for us to ever detect this occurrence. The reason for the difficulty is that DNA undergoes changes and mutations—some random and others through heritable epigenetic feedback loops. After even one million years the traces of any genetic engineering might become extremely hard to identify.

However, if advanced aliens wanted to leave a signature of their handiwork—a DNA calling card of sorts—they certainly could do this. There are some specific requirements if they want to prevent corruption by evolutionary mutations. If you want a signature to remain in DNA, or a fully fledged message, it needs to be encoded in regions of the genome that are extremely stable. The code that changes the least is generally the most important for essential basic functions of an organism. Scientists refer to these elements of code as highly conserved or even ultra-conserved. Most of the highly conserved genetic material is in noncoding DNA regions (once called junk DNA). It is possible for some sequences of DNA letters to remain stable over many tens of millions of years.

Samuel Arbesman, PhD, a computational biologist, has considered the subject of potential hidden messages in our genome. Arbesman explains that any modified area must be both highly conserved and essential to an organism's survival. This is the only way to be relatively certain that the encoded message would be passed down until life reached sufficiently high complexity to access the message. Keep in mind that any DNA that is not useful to the organism is almost certain to mutate.[3]

Here is a question to consider: What do chickens and chimpanzees have in common?

If we were to simply look at these two wildly divergent species, we would assume the answer to our question is *not much*. Moving below the level of form, you might be surprised to find chimps and chickens share some almost identical regions of DNA. One of these overlapping segments of code consists of 118 letters and differs by just two letters between these species. Two letters have mutated in species separated by three hundred million years of divergent evolution. Talk about stability.

When we come to contrast the same section of code in humans, a shock awaits us. Despite chimps being our closest living relative and separated by a mere six million years, we find a shocking eighteen-letter difference. From what has been unraveled so far by geneticists, it seems this segment—designated HAR1—plays a role in the development of the pattern and layout in the cerebral cortex. This is the folded gray matter understood to play a pivotal role in human consciousness.

It might be possible for readers to hear all this and miss the enormity. Sometimes when we read about discoveries in a scientific field that we don't thoroughly understand, there is a sense of "so what?" Let's just keep in mind that until hominins parted ways from the ancestors of chimpanzees, the rate of successful mutations in HAR1 was a single letter per 150 million years. This means that, in almost all cases where a natural copying error occurred, the impact was so severe that the affected offspring either died in utero or was so severely handicapped it failed to successfully reproduce. Yet, here we are with eighteen successful "mutations" in a fraction of that vast timescale, some arising just in the last few hundred thousand years. According to biostatistician Katherine Pollard, PhD, of the Gladstone Institute, "The fact that HAR1 was essentially frozen in time through hundreds of millions of years indicates that it does something very important; that it then underwent abrupt revision in humans suggests that this function was significantly modified in our lineage."[4]

What, then, could possibly bring about eighteen successful modifications to such a stable region of code, in fewer than six million years?

You are probably wondering what the academic view is on how known evolutionary mechanisms could bring about such a radical change. The best person to ask is the discoverer of these poorly understood human accelerated regions (HARs), Pollard, who says, "Statistically speaking, the probability that a highly conserved DNA sequence will change multiple times over 6 million years of evolution is close to zero."[5]

Pollard knows how to crunch the numbers: her area of expertise is the development of statistical and computational methods for use in the analysis of genomic datasets. There is nothing among known evolutionary mechanisms and environmental forces that would bring about such drastic changes without killing the organism. As we have discussed, the stability of these areas is essential to survival.

Even with this glaring anomaly, we might be tempted to assume a freak natural event is the actual cause, until we learn that several hundred human-specific accelerated regions of DNA code have been identified by scientists. While the vast majority of HARs remain entirely mysterious in function, it's understood that most of them tend to modify the development of the fetus. The majority of these regions are not inside genes but the switches that control gene expression (modifying the degree of expression or turning the genes on and off).

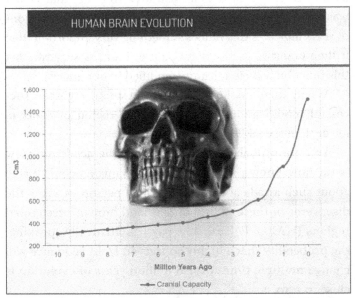

Chart depicts cranial expansion in line with body size and anomalous acceleration separate from body size changes after 800,000 years ago until present.

Researchers involved in the study of HARs suspect that the most profound differences between humans and their closest primate relatives are the result of these anomalous variations in highly conserved regions of code. Astonishingly, and beyond any reasonable coincidence, more than half of the genes located near HARs are involved in brain development and functioning. This is not a random scattering of sporadic mutations found distributed across the genome—not at all.

We find evidence in the fossil record marking a sudden acceleration in the human brain size and structure at two specific points: one about 1.8 million years ago and a second close to 780,000 years ago. Though HAR research is in the early stages, I am expecting to find a close correlation with the brain size acceleration events.

In the accounts provided by Alcheringa and within the many past life memories, we are told that after the destruction of the mothership, the marooned survivors abandoned the plan to colonize Earth. It became evident that without all the advanced technologies onboard the mothership they could not survive for very long in the hostile environment. The group discussed how to move forward. Eventually, they decided that the best direction would be to accelerate the evolution of the resident hominins and nudge them in a preferred direction. One of the sets of past life memories involved the individual recalling events from the perspective of one of the "enemy" beings that had switched sides: "The star people realise that the only way they can continue as a people on the Earth is to interbreed with an existing species that are able to thrive here. They choose the little hairy ones, a species we ourselves created."[6]

It should be mentioned here that the earth hominins had purportedly been engineered from more primitive primates long before the arrival of the mission from the Pleiades. These early human forms had been under the dominance of the resident hostile extraterrestrial species.

In other circumstances, the benevolent entities would perhaps not have interfered with the development of an indigenous species, knowing the profound impact this would have on their progression. In the situation of the upstanding ape, this creature had itself already been artificially engineered. The hominins had lived in the presence of an alien race since their beginning. Under these circumstances, there was no guiding principle broken by taking direct action and modifying the creature's future potential.

Valerie Barrow's work provides a considerable discussion of the events preceding and the first attempts to "upgrade" the hominins. With only limited medical and technological equipment, it was by no means easy. The engineering involved modifications at the genomic level as well as splicing of genetic material from other species, including the star people themselves.

The resulting "test-tube babies" were then implanted into a group of hominin mothers as well as several volunteers among the remaining female extraterrestrials. Some of the alien volunteers had a reproductive system rather closer to that of marsupials than mammals. This experimental process took time to perfect, and in some, heart-breaking failures are described. Valerie writes: "Many of us had been artificially impregnated with our own seed that had been genetically modified to produce a new being, able to cope with the sun and atmosphere of this place. More important, the newborn would be of the light."[7]

This is without a doubt the most essential aspect of Alcheringa's downloads that we have been able to validate. It's confirmation that humans have direct ancestry to both ancestral primates and advanced alien genetic engineers. The first ancestor of our *Homo sapiens* lineage was a hybrid creature resulting from an alien intervention. This ancestry makes us a unique organism on this planet, even when considering that all life here began with alien-seeded DNA. With this claimed uniqueness in mind, we should not be surprised that there are notable and anomalous differences separating us from our closest primate relatives.

The gold standard for identification of extraterrestrial genetic material in the human genome would be to contrast a human sample against reference material extracted from aliens. To the best of my knowledge, no such sample exists—unless it is in some deep black project somewhere. We could also identify a sudden anomalous addition if we compared *Homo sapiens'* DNA samples with those from hominins living eight hundred thousand years ago or more. Unfortunately, the oldest human DNA recovered is just 430,000 years old.

There is hope that one day we will recover suitably old hominin DNA for contrasting against the modern human genome. There has already been successful sequencing of 735,000-year-old samples from an extinct horse species. Ludovic Orlando, PhD, is one of the evolutionary geneticists that sampled the ancient horse DNA. Orlando believes that if fossils are well preserved by cold conditions, we might successfully sequence genomes from samples up to 1.5 million years old.[8]

As we do not have genetic material from an alien or from suitably ancient hominins, we must focus on identifying further fingerprints. We know that all life on Earth began with simple single-celled organisms and over time evolved toward greater complexity. Part of the evolutionary process involves mutations occurring and accruing over time until new species diverge. It takes considerable time for evolution to create new forms.

Assuming humans were fairly recently modified, as the evidence already suggests, there should be indications of us being a relatively new species. We should not have the same genetic depth of ancestry that other primates have. This is the case; in fact, chimpanzees limited to Africa have more genetic diversity than all seven billion humans spread across the planet.

Biologists place our split from the common ancestor shared with chimps at five or six million years ago. This allows for more than enough time for substantial genetic differences to develop among the members of both lineages. We would expect these levels to be very much alike. All living humans have virtually identical DNA, differing by only 0.1 percent. Our closest living genetic relatives, the chimpanzees, have about 1.2 percent variation in their genomes. This is an oddity; our species lacks the predicted depth of ancestry typical among related mammalian species.[9]

The absence of those significant intragroup differences is our first confirmation that *Homo sapiens* have a strange emergence story. The low level of genetic diversity suggests that our ancestors were members of a small isolated group that emerged within the last one million years.

We have already touched on the suggestion that the first *Homo sapiens* were engineered in Australia. We should quickly explore evidence that at least one group of early hominins reached Australia sufficiently early for this initial encounter. Although the aliens had their small saucer craft, there is no mention of having to collect humans from elsewhere. Recent archaeology has confirmed that early hominins including *Homo erectus* and the small, hairy *Homo floresiensis* were moving through the Indonesian islands by one million years ago.[10] It is logical that after crossing the Wallace Line, the geological divide between mainland Asia and Australasia, these hominins should have ended up in Australia. Evidence supportive of just such a migration has been identified in modern human DNA.

If a small group of early hominins splintered from those living across the vast Eurasian continent and moved to Australia, this would cause some initial loss of genetic diversity. A recent study has determined that our ancestors lost almost half their biological diversity about 1.2 million years ago, give or take three hundred thousand years.[11]

The date range for this event fits very well with the human archaeology found to the east of the Wallace Line. I have written more extensively about this in my book *The Forgotten Exodus: The Into Africa Theory of Human Evolution.* Mainly, any small human population isolated in a new land with an entirely novel ecology would be under unique evolutionary pressures. Beneficial changes in the genetic profile would also spread rapidly and be conserved.

We really want to establish when *Homo sapiens* started to diverge from their last hominin ancestor. To understand this, we need to look at some very recent findings. Geneticists have sequenced DNA from the fossils of Denisovans, Neanderthals, and early modern humans. This ancient DNA allowed them to calculate when these three human subspecies last shared a last common ancestor (LCA). The investigation into the LCA calculated a divergence date close to 750,000 years ago.[12]

Several years before the University of Utah team came to this early divergence date, a team from the Lawrence Berkeley National Laboratory traced one specific Neanderthal gene's evolutionary history. The team found that the genomic sequence had shared a most recent common ancestor with the reference modern human sequence approximately 770,000 years ago.[13]

Specific beta-globin sequences (blood proteins) identified in modern Asian populations descend from an archaic hominin ancestor of modern humans living about eight hundred thousand years ago.[14]

Without laboring the point, there are multiple lines of evidence pointing to the divergence of the first *Homo sapiens* from the LCA, very close to 780,000 years ago. We can now see that humans have a somewhat anomalous evolutionary beginning and that the timing matches the destruction of the extraterrestrial vessel and the other significant events. The next step in this analysis involves considering some of the specific differences that separate us from chimpanzees. I am not talking about the noticeable physical differences—morphology—here; we will talk about those later. Right now, we want to see if there is anything else strange lurking in our genetic makeup.

CHAPTER 13

FINGERPRINTS OF OUR ANCIENT ALIEN GENETIC ENGINEERS

I would rather be a transformed ape
than a degenerate son of Adam.

—PAUL PIERRE BROCA, anthropologist

One thing not only widens the gap between humans and all living primates but also brings us closer to our human cousins the Neanderthals and Denisovans. We are talking about the peculiar fusion of chromosome 2.

All primates except for modern humans, Neanderthals, and Denisovans have forty-eight chromosomes as twenty-four associated pairs. All living humans today have twenty-three pairs of chromosomes (aside from those with chromosomal disorders). Human chromosome 2 exhibits evidence of an end-to-end fusion involving two ancestral chromosomes. The exact mechanism through which these two archaic primate chromosomes evaded their protective telomeres (features at the end of chromosomes that prevent fusions) is not yet completely understood. It seems no genes from the end of the ancestral chromosomes 2A and 2B were lost during the fusing.[1]

The fact that Denisovans and Neanderthals share this chromosome fusion with us means it occurred before the divergence of these subspecies, in a shared ancestor.[2] We know this sets the minimum date at close to 780,000 years ago, but we also want information on the maximum age. To find out if the chromosome fusion happened close to the time humans split from Neanderthals or nearer to our divergence from ancestral primates, we need to turn to an expert.

Fortunately, I managed to track down the work of Adam Benton, a PhD student of human evolution at the University of Liverpool. Benton had asked a similar question about the fusion of these chromosomes. As an evolutionary scientist, Benton knew what to look for that could narrow down the timing of the fusion event.

The first assumption is that, though we have twenty-three pairs of chromosomes, our primate ancestors would have had twenty-four pairs, just as do all living primates; this isn't only possible inference, as there is visible evidence. Right in the middle of chromosome 2, scientists can see where one chromosome ended and another began.

As explained earlier, there is a lack of ancient DNA from the time when *Homo sapiens* first began to emerge. The oldest samples are only 430,000 years old. This is long after the fusion event occurred. Lacking ancient reference material, Benton took a straightforward look at the DNA structure itself. First, he explains how things work at that microscopic level. He then explains that DNA code consists of four nucleotides, which are linked letters A, C, G, and T. These letters are coded in pairs, with C and G naturally pairing, and A and T naturally pairing. Benton goes on to explain that these are not equal pairings: A and T are linked by two hydrogen bonds, whereas C and G have three. This means that C and G have a stronger relationship and, all else being equal, C and G are more likely to replace A and T rather than the reverse.

If a change to C and G breaks a gene, this invalidates the additional strength of the bonding; the related mutation is then discarded. In isolated cases, about 3 percent of these substitutions involve swapping of A and T for C and G. When we look at the entire human genome, substitution rates tend to approximately equalize. Benton highlights the fact that this bias occurs most actively where chromosomes exchange material through recombination, such as the ends of chromosomes. The fusion site on chromosome 2 displays the bias toward C and G even though it's no longer at the end of a chromosome so is not being excessively recombined. Now exempted from this bias for a considerable period, it has slightly less C and G than the tips of the chromosome.

In Benton's calculations, this fused region has been exempted from excessive recombination for at least 750,000 years. We already know the fusion is represented in Neanderthals and Denisovans, which means it occurred before the split. This gives a maximum and minimum dating centered on 780,000 years ago. In simple terms, the fusion of chromosome 2 happened at the time of the *Homo sapiens* lineage splitting away from their more archaic hominin ancestor.[3]

With the date of this fusion event matched, you might think we are done. How likely is it that this happened by chance at this pivotal time? Could this really be unrelated to all the other profound anomalies at that point in time? It certainly seems unlikely to be yet another mind-bending coincidence.

Some people will deem it unnecessary to go more in depth, but this is a profound revelation and the claims hold great importance. We must establish extraterrestrial directed modification beyond any reasonable doubt.

One point that must be addressed is whether the fusion event occurred several times among different populations, with convergent evolution separately producing similar results. Researchers have determined that all living people have the chromosome fusion at precisely the same site. This lack of variation tells us it happened just once in our shared ancestor.

The next area of investigation concerns the result of the fusion and how it became so prevalent among humans. Some scientists, especially those who believe in the Christian position of Creationism, have thrown tough questions at the details of the chromosome 2 fusion event. Robert W. Carter, PhD, a biologist, points out that chromosomal fusions, fissions, duplications, and rearrangements are most often adverse events for an organism. It is very rare that spontaneous chromosome fusions are neutral and even less often do they bring any positive changes. Chromosomal fusion is one primary cause of infertility, and indeed, most embryos with such a drastic error tend to be spontaneously aborted by the mother's body.[4]

As a sporadic mutation, the fusion of chromosome 2 should have occurred in just one individual in a single generation. Even with the fetus beating the odds and maturing to a live birth, this aberration should have soon vanished again, absorbed into a larger population of people with forty-eight chromosomes.

Let's speculate and say that perhaps several offspring were produced by a single male impregnating several females. Perhaps half of the resulting children might carry the mutation. This gives the potential for second-generation couplings where the fusion might be present. We would expect at most to end up with a small population of people with forty-six chromosomes alongside a majority with forty-eight. It is statistically doubtful two children with the same mutation would be produced even by the same parents. This also assumes the mutation is not negative in its impact.

The reality is that, as best as can be deduced from evidence, all the earliest ancestors of *Homo sapiens* living 780,000 years ago and onward had forty-six chromosomes. Scientists can't offer a definitive answer for why this would be, but they have made some suggestions. One model argues that this fusion event happened within a small, isolated ancestral population, allowing it to be spread rapidly across the entire group. The second model offered assumes that the fusion event brought with it some immense benefits that provided enormous evolutionary advantages to carriers. Many biologists feel that to become dominant across the globe in all humans, the fusion of chromosome 2 must have occurred in a small, isolated ancestral population and additionally provided extraordinary benefits.

This fusion event has the fingerprints of the alien scientists all over it. The pattern we see matches well with a deliberate scientific experiment involving a group of isolated hominins implanted with modified test-tube babies. There would have been an entire generation of potential breeding pairs carrying this fusion.

In one science article I read, the author mentioned that there appeared to be a somewhat-fortuitous concurrent genetic mutation that would have acted to prevent a spontaneous miscarriage of the mutated fetuses. How incredibly fortunate!

In many respects, the ideal situation would have been to work on a small regionally isolated population. This would make any hominins isolated in Australia perfect subjects. Australia has been ecologically separated from the rest of the world for millions of years. The difficulty in reaching Australasia led to a wide range of globally unique species. Famous physicist Michio Kaku, PhD, has spoken on the fact that any humans isolated in Australia's unique ecosystem would have experienced accelerated evolutionary adaptations. Such a population would also be cut off from any "normalizing" gene flow from other human populations ranging between Africa and Eurasia. For all these reasons it would make it very likely that beneficial new mutations would rapidly be passed on to the entire local population.[5]

We can't help but wonder what the benefits of genetic engineering might have been. What was the result of these new humans? The aim of the genetic engineering project was to create a superior species. We know that this new creature eventually managed to outcompete or absorb all the hominins on Earth. That is impressive and further suggests a fantastic result from the modification process.

Manuel Ruiz Rejón of Granada University in Spain explains that "there is a possibility that the chromosome fusion that originated our chromosome-2 may have been associated with the appearance of our distinctive characteristics."[6] Ruiz Rejón highlights various genes in human chromosome 2 that are positioned close to the fusion site. These genes are expressed more intensely in humans than in any large apes. These same genes are expressed in highly significant tissues and organs, including the brain and the gonads. Ruiz Rejón also speculated that the loss of specific DNA sequences resulting from the fusion might also have had positive effects on human ancestors. It could be that the problem-causing sequences were cleaned up; perhaps we were on our way to extinction?[7]

The fusion site of chromosome 2 is positioned in a highly unusual location, being on the intron of a gene. It is considered very rare for fusions to occur on the intron of functional genes. This begs the questions: Which gene is it and what functions does it have?

The gene in question is DDX11L2, and it expresses itself in cells performing tasks for the nervous, muscular, immune, and reproductive systems. Those are rather crucial areas that an alien scientist would want to influence. The fusion site also contains a DNA sequence that changes how the gene will be expressed, what is known as a transcription factor binding site.[8]

With the mention of genes associated with the human brain connected to the chromosome 2 fusion, we can't help but wonder what was done in that respect. Indeed, any upgrade to the human species would involve giving it superior intelligence. It should be considered a red flag for meddling if we can identify sudden beneficial changes in our brain structure at the time of this fusion event. So, do we see any noticeable changes in the human brain about 780,000 years ago?

The short answer is yes—lots. For several decades evolutionary scientists have been investigating the sudden mysterious acceleration of human brain size that began close to eight hundred thousand years ago. This date was estimated from changes in fossil human skulls that had been collected from around the planet.

This shift began a period of unprecedented brain evolution that continued until two hundred thousand years ago.[9] Before this point in time, our brain size had been increasing in step with body size. This acceleration in brain size is peculiar in evolutionary terms.[10] Rapidly enlarging brains requires considerable additional energy to be diverted from other functions, including muscles. Rapidly weakening muscles is a problematic trade-off for brain expansion, during a period when creatures fought tooth and claw to survive.

We also need to appreciate that any increase in skull size requires adaptive modification in the width of the birth canal. The sudden emergence of significantly larger heads would clash directly with the limitations of the human pelvis. This change would undoubtedly lead to a very high mortality rate for both mothers and babies. It could potentially usher in an extinction event. When you ponder those negative factors, it becomes evident that a rapidly expanding brain comes with hugely negative implications. It is questionable whether this is an immediately positive change.

We return to these problems later and examine some strange changes in early humans that prevented potential extinction because of the upgrades. For the moment let's just focus on a few specific genes that seem to have been part of the modification of the human brain. The first gene of note is called ARHGAP11B, a gene discovered to be highly active within the human neural progenitor cells but entirely absent from examined mouse cells. Marta Florio, a molecular and cellular biologist at the Max Planck Institute, explains that this tiny snippet of DNA, just 804 letters long, is actually a short segment from a longer gene. The research team were left baffled. It appeared that this gene had been chopped up and the fragment duplicated before being reinserted into the human genome. This is something scientists are doing today with so-called CRISPR gene editing technologies—but not something we would expect to see occurring hundreds of thousands of years ago.[11]

This same gene, ARHGAP11B, seems to be uniquely human, though it has not been found in our primate relatives. Very notably, this crucial sliver of code is located in the genome of both Neanderthals and Denisovans. This tells us the replication and insertion happened before the now-well-dated split between these human populations.

The gene ARHGAP11B invokes the neocortex to contain many more neurons. The neocortex is the most recently evolved section of the brain (hence the prefix *neo-*, meaning "new"). Some scientists suspect this tiny snippet of DNA laid the foundation for the human brain's massive expansion. The human neocortex has distinctive folds that allow for far greater information processing than possible with a large but smooth brain.

Many genes are unique to humans, further separating us from primates. Most of these relate to our complex brain structure. Another such gene plays a crucial role in human brain development: miR-941. This gene is highly active in brain regions controlling decision-making and enabling language abilities. The study of miR-941 has caused researchers to speculate that its involvement in advanced higher brain functions is fundamental to making us human.

This gene, miR-941, emerged fully functional out of noncoding DNA in a very brief evolutionary event. Though the emergence date has been suggested at perhaps one million years ago, we know that it preceded the divergence of Denisovans, as they also carry this gene. Listening to the opinions of one member of the miR-941 research project, Martin Taylor of the University of Edinburgh, we get the impression he suspects that it appeared alongside the sudden rapid brain growth 780,000 years ago. Taylor explains that the gene "sprang from nowhere at a time when our species was undergoing dramatic changes."[12]

Perhaps one of the most commonly known human genes is FOXP2, implicated in the emergence of human language abilities. Researchers from MIT and several European universities have shown that the human version of the gene makes it easier to transform new experiences into routine procedures. The FOXP2 protein sequence is very strongly conserved in mammalian evolution. Human FOXP2 differs by two amino acids from that of chimpanzees, gorillas, and macaques, all of which have identical sequences. These two amino acid fixations are rather unlikely to manifest by chance random mutation alone.

The initial changes in the FOXP2 transcriptional factor occurred after the split from our primate relatives but before the divergence of Neanderthals and Denisovans. Neuroscientists have found that further mutations occurred in this gene about two hundred thousand years ago. These changes enhanced synaptic connectivity and adaptability in neural circuitry. It is widely believed to play a significant role in our ability to produce and understand speech.[13]

Professor Garry Nolan is exploring links between human intuition and the caudate-putamen structures in the basal ganglion of the brain. Nolan has found a reason to suspect that the size of these structures impacts intuitive abilities. Incredibly, FOXP2 is also found to express in the development of the caudate and putamen. Could it be that our extraterrestrial benefactors wanted us to be able to effectively communicate through both speech and some form of higher psychical exchange?[14]

The study of the many HARs is still in its relatively early stages, and there will be many more revelations to come. Two things that seem unlikely to change are the extraordinary nature of these alterations and the type of language academics are forced to use in discussing them.

As our own science of genetic engineering moves forward, we are starting to understand that it is not all about hybridization and gene splicing. Inevitably we are heading more toward directing the expression of genes. Once we can map out and understand the DNA code that acts as the switches for genetic expression, we will be able to absolutely shape the human organism. No doubt such experimentation inevitably involves terrible mistakes and horrific failings.

There is no single gene for the magnificent thing that is the human brain, but a great many genes have roles to play. To make a beneficial change of significant magnitude requires modifying the degree to which these genes express in our biological makeup. We can now look at the hundreds of anomalous human-specific accelerations from a position of revised understanding. Astonishing changes in our neurology manifested only after the split from chimps. It is in these changes we recognize the handiwork of master geneticists. These were scientists not only light-years from home but also light-years ahead.

Humanity has just begun the genetic revolution as we start to utilize powerful tools like directed horizontal gene transfer and CRISPR/Cas9 gene editing tools. The precision modification available through CRISPR opens astonishing possibilities, and it may be the distant precursor of the tools used by the extraterrestrials. More recently, CRISPR gene drives have come into use—tools that force genes to spread through an entire population. When one parent carries the CRISPR gene drive, it cuts out the other parent's gene and replaces it with the desired copy. This type of technology fits very well with the observation that the modified humans rapidly replaced all preexisting hominin types. This would readily explain why anomalous changes like the fusion of chromosome 2 became ubiquitous.[15]

Even with a small starting population, once the gene drive is unleashed, the modifications will inevitably spread to every organism in the target species. Early *Homo sapiens* could have interbred with *Homo erectus,* and in every case the child would assuredly be a new *Homo sapiens.* Gene-drive technology can even be used to engineer the assured extinction of any target species.

When all known natural evolutionary mechanisms are factored in, and the numbers are crunched, there is a statistical chance of zero that all these many genetic anomalies should exist. Yet, there they are: fingerprints of the star gods, a cosmic message in a biological bottle.

While some will say that we can't prove aliens did all this, I would counter that science does not work that way. Few things in scientific exploration are proven beyond any doubt. Scientists are compelled to accept and utilize the most robust models—the working hypothesis that best explains the observed evidence. The academics should provide a stronger argument and offer a superior explanation.

Right now, the only scientific explanation that immediately makes sense of all HARs and other associated genetic anomalies would be an unnatural intervention. Some force overcame all of the usual mechanics of evolution, upending essential genomic stability—without killing us. We know of only one such force in the universe: intelligence.

CHAPTER 14

THE CHILDREN OF EARTH

*The human baseline of creative cooperation, the ability
to think, communicate, and collaborate with increasing
prowess, transformed us into beings who invented the
technologies that support domestication, economies,
large-scale societies, warfare, and broad-scale peace.*

—PROFESSOR AGUSTIN FUENTES, anthropologist

C reating an "upgraded" human species with higher brain
capacity would inevitably involve some enormous chal-
lenges. One of the most immediate is how to get a significantly larger head to fit through the existing narrow birth
canal. If all subsequent generations of babies cause the
death of mothers in childbirth, the experiment would soon
end in an extinction event. It appears that the alien scientists came up with an ingenious workaround for this problem: they altered the growth cycle of the fetus so that birth
would occur before full development to infancy.

The majority of mammal fetuses develop to a high
degree of maturity in the womb before birth. This provides the advantage of young animals being able to reach
a reasonable level of self-sufficiency in a remarkably short
time following delivery. A great many mammals produce

young able to walk within hours of birth, and within a few weeks they are able to supplement mother's milk with the food they forage for themselves. Mobility also allows young animals to potentially evade predators or flee from other dangers. If we look at horses, for example, we can see that a foal walks almost immediately, grows to its near-adult height and size (about 80 percent of this) within a year or so, and then enters puberty by about age two. After about four years the foal is an adult horse and will likely live into its twenties, all being well.

Things could not be more different for human babies and the development stages they pass through. Human infants are born while still in their fetal stages of development. We can observe this in the fact that the bones of the skull have not yet fused and in the lack of spinal strength; they can't even safely support the weight of their own heads. Our offspring are incredibly dependent on their mothers for sustenance. It takes a further six months for the infant's neck muscles to become sufficiently strong and for the first attempts at crawling to begin. All the while, the human brain growth continues at an incredibly rapid pace. If we return to our foal for a moment, we can expect to see it walk or run within a few hours of birth.

Being born as a fetus allows our species to have a lengthy period of rapid brain expansion beyond the womb, sparing a mother from additional pain or extremely high chances of death during childbirth.

It must be pointed out here that human mothers still must go through the most painful and dangerous birthing process of all mammals. While evolution favors low-risk, easy deliveries, humans have a one in one thousand chance of bearing a child too large to pass through the birth canal.[1] Almost all instances of human childbirth require some level of assistance and with it a painful process. Most of the apes and monkeys give birth within two hours, whereas first time human mothers will suffer for an average of nine hours. Clearly, something went very wrong with the standard evolutionary winnowing out through natural selection, reversing many of the gains made by our primate ancestors!

After a longer pregnancy than other primates, our offspring then has a substantially elongated infancy. Walking takes about eighteen months to unfold, and speech typically begins at approximately two years of age. The first words come concurrently with the fusing of the bones of the skull. This marks the end of the fetal stage, throughout which children are astonishingly vulnerable. Then begins an incredibly long stretch of childhood with continued parental dependency.

While every child is slightly different, no child will be physically mature and become capable of sexual reproduction until somewhere between ten and sixteen years of age. This infertility is partly a protective function, as a small-framed young female has a very high chance of death during childbirth. This slow maturation is hardly beneficial to increasing the active population. Within this same period, many of our fellow mammals have completed their entire life cycles, having produced dozens of offspring. Many mammals will be already heading into their senior years and physical decline. Even after all these years have passed, a human is not fully developed either physically or psychologically. They are finally just capable of keeping themselves alive.

Humans are what they are today primarily because of this greatly elongated maturation period. The correct term for this stretched childhood is *neoteny*. I imagine many readers probably haven't heard of neoteny as it is not a widely discussed subject outside of academic circles. It is, of course, related to the better-known term *neonatal*. It relates to infant development—or, more specifically, the retention of juvenile features in an adult animal. Neoteny also refers to the sexual maturity of an animal while it is still in a mainly larval state. The term *pedogenesis* also applies to the same phenomenon.

Perhaps the best-known example of a highly neotenic creature is the Mexican axolotl. The axolotl is essentially a larval salamander that can breed while still in its juvenile form and does not usually ever mature into the adult body type. Though the axolotl looks physically very different from salamanders, at the DNA level, they are identical.

Scientists have discovered that larval salamanders require iodine to trigger maturation. In the region where the axolotl lives, there is a lack of iodine in the pools in which the young are hatched. It appears that at some time in the past some of the young creatures adapted to their problematic environments through becoming fertile without ever becoming a land-dwelling salamander. Some axolotls, a tiny minority, eventually crawl out of their pools and become adults.

One common reason why a great many people have a knee-jerk dismissal reaction when they are told modern humans evolved from an apelike primate is that we just look so incredibly different from living primates. The physical, morphological differences are then added to the extreme behavioral differences between apes and humans. There is a sense of us being a wildly different species. The truth is that there are both extremely close links among all primates, including us, and yet also some profound differences.

It is often said that we share almost 99 percent of our DNA with chimps. This emerged from a flawed contrasting of the genomes of the two species. We have to look at the various mutations, segment repeats, and section omissions and which genes are currently expressing or are turned off. Once that is carried out the high figure can be revised downward quite considerably, to perhaps less than 95 percent. Where it really counts, in genetic expression, humans are profoundly different from chimps. So, what about our unique looks?

Once we move beyond primary anatomical overlaps, humans look very unlike chimpanzees; we can all plainly see this with our own eyes. If we are fellow primates, essentially an unusually large-brained form of bipedal ape, why do we look so different?

The answer to how modern humans acquired their strange appearance can be found in an exploration of the neotenic process. Look again at chimpanzees, specifically the head profile of infant chimps. The resemblance to a human child is stunning. Some of our features, including a disproportionately large head, rounded skull, flat face, lack of thick body hair, and several other traits, are common between humans and infant chimpanzees. It becomes clear that we are something strangely alike to the axolotl. Human beings are an ape stuck in its infant form throughout life.

We can even see that our face is now flatter than it once was because we still grow too many teeth for the size of our jaw. Most people do not have straight teeth and a great many need to have teeth removed to allow others to grow correctly. This is because we have lost the protruding lower jaw typical of adult apes. Evolution of the mouth has not yet caught up with the sudden flattening of our face. Eventually humans will likely stop producing wisdom teeth.

Significant neoteny in humans began around the time that the first members of our genus, *Homo*, emerged, sometime between two and three million years ago.[2] This initial phase of neoteny increased the maturation period and allowed for the size of the human brain to expand, even if only gradually. We might recall that Alcheringa tells us that the first archaic humans were created by a rival extraterrestrial species. It is likely this first neotenic shift was related to their engineering of the *Homo* genus.

Academics have found that at the start of the *Homo* genus there was an incomplete segmental duplication of the ancestral gene SRGAP2. This event produced a new gene, SRGAC2, which slowed spine maturation and allowed for more neuronal migration. The new gene had a drastic effect on dendrite spines, anatomical substrate involved in memory storage and synaptic transmission. Perhaps this also increased potential contacts among neurons in the brain. The mutation resulted in higher synaptic densities in humans when compared to other primates.

Geneticists studying SRGAC2 found that during the aging process about 48 percent of the genes involved in the development of the prefrontal cortex change differently in humans and chimpanzees. The summary offered is that a "significant excess of genes" related to the development of the prefrontal cortex show "neotenic expression in humans" relative to chimpanzees. The notable contrast between these species is best explained by the neoteny hypothesis of human evolution: that we are primarily a neotenic ape.[3]

The second round of genetic engineering was aimed at far more than the creation of a simple-minded servile hominin species. It would have made sense for these beings to drastically accelerate the process of neoteny in humans. Not only was this required to allow us our larger brains without dying in childbirth, but it fundamentally changed behavior.

It is worth mentioning that the retention of the subtle body hairs typical of a late-stage ape's fetus would enable humans to rapidly lose excess heat. Overheating is a potential problem for large-brained creatures, as brains burn a lot of calories for neural processes.

Neoteny also had implications for the psychological makeup of humans. Infants have more cognitive flexibility. They learn many new skills concurrently, use abstract thinking, and have beautiful leaps of imagination. The brain of a child is hardwired toward curiosity, prompts a thirst for learning, and has powerful information absorption capabilities. The neural networks are very plastic and flexible while we are young; they continually rewire to suit new tasks. Infants specialize in replicating observed behavior. They must if they are to mature. One distinct characteristic of young animals is the desire to play. Extreme playfulness can be observed in the offspring of almost any mammalian species.

Adult animals typically become very stuck in their ways. They specialize in a skill set and then fixate on repeating a small number of essential activities. Adults across the animal kingdom are generally not very interested in play and instead focus almost exclusively on building a home, finding mates, raising their young, and foraging for food.

By retaining a childlike brain structure into adulthood, humans became perhaps the most mentally flexible and environmentally adaptive species on Earth. Many typical adult human psychological characteristics (such as our incredible curiosity, playfulness, overt displays of affection, and indeed much of our complex social behavior) are products of neoteny.

Substantial social implications also accompanied increased neoteny. In a species in which infants can walk and gather food soon after birth, there is less requirement for adults to dedicate time and energy to child-rearing. Producing highly independent young reduces the need for an adult to engage in communal living or utilize complex social behavior; moving in groups is merely a way to increase protection from predators and improves the chances of locating food sources.

The lengthy total dependence of human infants on their mothers and their incredible vulnerability make it almost impossible for them to survive to adulthood without help from an extended family grouping. If we imagine a lone mother with her baby having to gather enough food for milk production over many months, while continually holding that baby, it becomes apparent this would be incredibly impractical. This mother would also need to defend herself and her infant against opportunistic predators. Humans are relatively weak; we have no horns, claws, or long fangs. Humans could defeat very few large, predatory animals in one-on-one unarmed combat.

A mother with a baby is both vulnerable and hindered in gathering food. She needs at least a mate willing to dedicate to helping her. The survival of a human child really requires the efforts of a large group in which food is communally sourced, resources shared, and many adult caregivers available. It is quite clear that our early ancestors would not have flourished as a species without communities.

In many respects neoteny represented the spark that led to human communities. Any sane mother wants her offspring to survive and will do what is best toward that aim. The best thing for a mother, then, is to find a partner with the same dedication, maintain close relationships with immediate family members, and form social contracts of mutual support with other adults.

We now know that much of our sizable complex brain is dedicated to processing information about other humans. There is considerable value in knowing about other people and how to best maintain an optimal position within a highly complicated group structure. Essentially our brains are hardwired for gossiping and social networking. No surprise, then, that even today most humans love both activities!

Evolutionary scientists have also deduced that many neotenous traits have been highly favored in mate selection. Women today have more neotenous features than males, having less body hair, smaller noses, larger eyes, flatter faces, and delicate jawlines. These and other childlike features have evidently attracted male partners and caused these traits to be reinforced. In fact, studies have shown men to prefer women with greater neoteny. Many typically neotenic features are found to be favored above those we often associate with sexual attraction, such as shapely bottoms and breasts. Consider that even a woman with an hourglass figure, long legs, and luscious long hair will still struggle to find an ideal mate if she grows chest hair and a full mustache and sports a prominent brow ridge or protruding square jaw. Regular adult ape features, such as those described, are not considered especially desirable in human females.

It is suspected that men's natural programming to help and protect children meant they tended to extend this more often to women with childlike features. Women would have selected men who had an active protective urge toward children. This strongly reinforced these traits in males. We can easily see how this creates a feedback loop and ensures that most successful interbreeding involves women with greater neoteny, and their genes will favor children (both female and male) with the same neotenic features.[4]

The process of increasing neoteny is also observed in some other species, especially domesticated animals. This is very intriguing because once our wild ancestors were taken into the genetic engineering and breeding program, they were mostly being tamed by the alien scientists. These apparently long-lived visitors to our planet were able to ensure several generations of interbreeding favoring traits they wanted. These scientists would also have prevented any potentially problematic inbreeding. This is very much how we have shaped animals such as dogs and horses over many generations of deliberate directing of bloodlines.[5]

It seems likely that once direct shepherding and intentional domestication came to an end, self-domestication took over. The preference for partners with a pro-social outlook would have ensured ongoing taming of human nature. The aliens may have gotten the domestication ball rolling, but we have kicked it all the way down the road. "One reason that made scientists claim that humans are self-domesticated lies within our behavior: modern humans are docile and tolerant, like domesticated species, our cooperative abilities and pro-social behavior are key features of our modern cognition," explains Professor Cedric Boeckx.[6]

The second reason for Boeckx claiming that self-domestication is evidenced in modern humans arises from contrasting us against Neanderthals. When modern humans are compared directly to Neanderthals, our sub-species has much more gracile morphology. The same is observed when we compare human-domesticated animals to their wild cousins. Recent studies have found that there is a statistically significant number of genetic overlaps between modern humans and various domesticated animals. This genetic signature for domestication was not observed in the Neanderthal genome. When we look at

Neanderthal morphology, it is clear they have fewer neotenous features than modern humans.

It starts to look as if Neanderthals went feral at some
stage in prehistory. They fragmented into small, isolated
family groups and lived wild, rugged lives. In taking a less-
domesticated path, Neanderthal morphology changed. The
indefinite childhood was being lost; they started to become
adult-form humans—more apelike.

It seems that what really separates these two human
groups is not so much divergence as behavioral changes.
Due to epigenetic effects, Neanderthal choices began to
impact gene expression. As our cousins abandoned complex social behavior, this reversed some of the associated
neotenic changes. It seems we really are quite literally the
product of our thinking and actions. Every action we take
right now and every idea we have are shaping not only ourselves but our descendants. We better decide now what we
want humans to be like in the future!

It must be said that there are negative aspects to being a
creature modified by advanced aliens, especially when they
have lost the bulk of their technology. There are some hor-
rendous DNA errors in the human genome that also make
us unique among primates. Human reproductive biology
really stands out in this context. Humans have the lowest
fertility rates and the highest child mortality rates of all
primates. Human females are unique in having no obvious
indicator of ovulation, a brief seventy-hour period of fertility per month. Approximately 7–12 percent of couples
experience reproductive troubles, often with severe impact
on their mental well-being.[7]

Low sperm count impacts 1–2 percent of men, and
25 percent of women suffer from failure to produce healthy
eggs. Even when conception does somehow successfully

occur, there are significant chances of failure to implant or failure of hormones that prevent uterine shedding. Also, if these problems are avoided, at least 10–25 percent of recognized pregnancies will end in spontaneous abortion within thirteen weeks. Miscarriage is usually due to a wide range of developmental disorders common to our species, many of which are ironically hereditary. In all, when pregnancy issues are calculated, up to 50 percent of zygotes don't make it more than a few weeks.

Miscarriages, stillbirths, and infant deaths are rare among our primate relatives. Modern humans have almost bridged the gap but only through stunning advances in medical intervention. Finally, with all the other potential issues overcome, it will likely take a couple of years of attempts to produce a single weak and vulnerable offspring. Prolific, successful reproduction is undoubtedly a crucial function for any organism, certainly in terms of evolutionary success. Our species seems to be almost engineered for reproductive failure in this respect. If you have ever felt like a reproductive failure, wondered if God has punished you, or just felt the stinging pain of a lost pregnancy, know that it is not your fault and you are far from alone. I have seen too many people blame themselves for what are species-wide troubles.

It may be that some of these troubles encouraged long-term paired relationships, but such pairings also occur among other, less-cursed species. It really is a wonder that we managed to evade extinction long enough to develop the advanced medicines and technologies that allowed our species to flourish. If the alien engineers show their faces, they will have some serious explaining to do.

CHAPTER 15

ALIENS AND THE ECOLOGICAL COLLAPSE

We are part of a symbiotic relationship
with something which disguises itself as an
extra-terrestrial invasion so as not to alarm us.

—TERENCE MCKENNA, ethnobotanist

I n a recent panel discussion on the search for extraterrestrial intelligence, leading space scientists touched on the potential link between discovering aliens and saving our planet. One astrobiologist on the panel, Caleb Scharf, began: "It's a bit of a stretch, but this is another motivation for finding other life in the universe."[1]

Scharf then theorized that perhaps events similar to the human story may have already played out many times before elsewhere in the cosmos. He feels that if scientists could investigate an alien civilization, even if only by remote observations of their planetary atmosphere, it could teach us about ecological mistakes they have made. "There are other stories out there, potentially, that could tell us how to do things and actually make it through this augmentation period or make it through a filter. There may be other places where it worked and places where it failed, and we can learn from that too," concluded Caleb.

Our planet is currently on a collision course with catastrophe. It does not seem coincidental that in many alien abductions or contact cases, the experiencer claims they were shown images of a global environmental disaster. The beings, or the intelligence, give dire warnings about the direction humanity has set itself upon. The most common theme among communications is a warning that our species must change course or face catastrophe.

The rapid pace of the unfolding disaster is frightening to comprehend—so much so that most people do everything they can to not think about it at all. Before I start to reel off grim statistics, let's begin by stating the obvious: the days of our global civilization are severely numbered, and it may even be that the number of future generations can be counted on our fingers. Earth is currently passing into the worst uptick in species die-offs since the destruction of the dinosaurs sixty-five million years ago, and their extinction involved a giant asteroid impact. It is considered normal for as many as five species to become extinct in any given year. Right now, we are losing species at a rate of several dozen per day, thousands of times faster than the natural speed. Scientific estimates suggest we may have as much as half of all life threatened with extinction by mid-century.

We have all heard of the floating islands of garbage in our oceans. These mounds of death ensnare everything from turtles and dolphins to birds and fish. There are already more than 165 million tons of plastic in the sea, and by about 2050 it is considered likely we will have more plastic in the seas than we will have fish. Let that sink in for a moment. It's not a comfortable picture.

The destruction of rainforests is old news. The desperate pleas to save "Earth's lungs" were sounded decades ago when I was just a young child, but not much has happened to stop the process. Rainforests once covered 14 percent of the earth's land surface, but human activity has reduced this to just 6 percent. Various experts in the field estimate the last rainforests could be consumed in under forty years.

In just the last few months a new aspect of the global meltdown has been featured in mainstream media. We are talking about the total collapse of insect populations across most of the planet. Scientists in Puerto Rican rainforests report 98 percent of ground insect life vanished; 80 percent of those are usually found in the tree canopy.

Reports from German nature reserves suggest a loss of 75 percent of local insect populations. Mexico's dry forests have lost up to 80 percent of their insect life in just over thirty years. By a large margin, habitat change such as deforestation, urbanization, and conversion to farmland were identified as the most significant cause of insect decline and extinction. I will save you the time needed to read the full list and summarize that this is a global phenomenon and a frightening one.[2]

You have probably never heard the scientific term *bottom-up trophic cascade*, but rest assured that shortly it will be mentioned much more frequently. Bottom-up trophic cascade refers to the inevitable effects of losing the bottom layer of the ecosystem chain. With the astonishing rate of insect extinction, it is unavoidable that larger animals usually dependent on insects for food will also die off.

It should not surprise you to hear that frogs and birds are vanishing from forests at an astonishing rate, with other insectivores following suit. Creatures that survive by eating a diet of insects and small insectivores are following their prey into the abyss. This presages a total ecosystem collapse; few animals will escape the inevitable consequences. Humanity may be a master of the planet, but even our intelligent species can't survive without its ecosystem. There is a long shadow being cast across our species: that of a tall figure clutching a scythe.

I have recently been talking with my friend Brian J. Noble, a retired science journalist and author of the book *How Will Our Children Survive*. Brian paints an equally grim picture of the near future, though his primary focus is on a very uniquely human problem. If you search for the stats on how much oil remains, about fifty years of reserves are projected. According to Brian's research, the actual figure is closer to thirty years, meaning there is insufficient time to allow any alternative energy to effectively replace oil.[3] Without oil, which ironically is helping to drive the environmental collapse, the industrial age will come to a crashing halt. The end of oil will bring unprecedented chaos, think *Mad Max*-level societal disarray.

While I am offering only a very brief snapshot of humanity's troubles, it should be enough to make any sensible person hold their head in their hands with despair. Our children or grandchildren will live in an unrecognizable world compared to the one we inherited. The next generation will face hardships that would have been unimaginable just a few decades ago. The generations that follow may not even be able to eke out an existence at all. We won't survive without our environmental support systems.

The party is over, and there is going to be no easy cure for the resulting hangover. The looming end of human civilization is, without doubt, the single biggest issue facing us, but it is also closely linked to the most intriguing question ever asked: Are we alone in the universe?

While there is some small hope that humanity can slam on the breaks and divert our train before it goes over the cliff, I imagine many of you reading this will share in my skepticism of this likelihood. We have a system that measures the positivity of the future on economic charts and a system built almost entirely on endless consumerism and exponential growth. It is an inconvenient fact for the business world that just one hundred companies are responsible for 71 percent of the emissions linked to climate change (and who knows how much other pollution).[4] Even as many individuals make better choices, the companies continue with business as usual. This reality leaves me pessimistic about the chances of humans solving this problem alone and in time to stave off a cataclysm.

If human-level thinking is doing a much better job at destroying the planet than saving it, perhaps if we had a nonhuman intelligence allied with us, we might be able to achieve the needed changes. If we had a human-engineered artificial intelligence to help organize the cleanup, that might be a useful start. That sounds good in principle, but the problem is we don't yet have a real "better than human," self-aware artificial intelligence in sight.

In fact, a survey conducted in 2016, involving 352 experts from various positions in the AI field, sought to determine when robots would be able to perform any task better than a human. The depressing results were that the average prediction placed this level of development just within fifty years.[5] The possibility that we will develop a true AI, capable of taking over logistical control of the mission to save the planet and in time to do so, really looks remote.

With real artificial intelligence too far off into the future to help save the planet and low expectations of an ingenious plan from the chimpanzees or dolphins, only one other nonhuman intelligence can help us: advanced extraterrestrial intelligence. Benevolent alien beings may be our last best hope for a bright future for human generations to come. We have already discovered that humans are not alone. There is somebody else in the game with us, whether they are physical organisms, a post-biological intelligence, or something even more bizarre. (Incidentally, my money is on the latter.)

To have any hope of establishing a knowledge and technology transfer from an elder race of space beings requires first that we can readily detect them and then make appropriate concerted efforts at contact. The evidence suggests that highly psychic people are the ideal medium for this task.

We will require scientists to be involved in such a process, especially those who understand both Earth's problems and its needs. It would take our greatest minds to work with any willing extraterrestrial or interdimensional intelligence to ensure that we followed them and used their help effectively. We would, of course, require governments to be involved in the provision of the logistical support and infrastructure needed by scientists.

We must face a glaring problem here: academics are the most skeptical people when it comes to the existence of advanced alien life. Our leading scientists are especially doubtful of the possibility that aliens have ever visited Earth, let alone that they are actively operating nearby. For an established academic to openly ponder the possibility that aliens not only exist but have contacted Earth can be career suicide. Considerable pressure is put on scientists to not say things that can be construed as either scientifically baseless or downright silly. We need a cultural shift that changes this unfortunate, and potentially dangerous, paradigm.

What must happen for leading scientists to engage with the search for advanced alien intelligence? And how can we encourage the right people to seek contact with an intelligence potentially able to save our species from imminent self-destruction?

The answers to these two questions are in working with the scientific method and recognizing the need for compelling objective evidence combined with falsifiable hypotheses. That is where the information in this book comes into play. We finally have solid scientific data that any relevant scientist can investigate. Falsifiable hypotheses can be explored and tested:

Alcheringa is either an alien intelligence embedded in an ancient artifact, or he never existed.

About 780,000 years ago, a giant crystalline ship exploded above Australia leaving debris, or another explanation can be found.

The *Homo sapiens* genome is either rife with strangely modified DNA code, or there is not a scrap of it to be found.

Something bizarre and worthy of study is happening to thousands of alien abductees, or they are all liars.

Senior military officers have acquired evidence of advanced technology, or they are running a malicious disinformation campaign.

Scientists in deep state projects have validated psychic powers, or they are just a bunch of cranks.

So, which is it?

These are all testable claims, and I offer them as hypotheses to the scientific community. These matters represent the multiple surfaces of a single core phenomenon. If I am right, and I am confident that's the case, then we are in the presence of a superintelligence that could help us avert extinction. Perhaps it simply awaits our full engagement and a request for assistance. Scientists certainly have nothing to lose in exploring the evidence. If they fail to do so, we may lose everything.

AFTERWORD

The symbolic display seen by the abductees is identical
to the type of initiation ritual or astral voyage that is
imbedded in the [occult] traditions of every culture . . .
the structure of abduction stories is identical to that
of occult initiation rituals . . . the UFO beings of today
belong to the same class of manifestation as the [occult]
entities that were described in centuries past.

—JACQUES VALLEE, PhD

There is no doubt in my mind that there is an alien presence sharing our mundane reality. I am quite confident that if more scientists were to focus their efforts on investigating the relevant evidence already provided, they would inevitably conclude the same. If anything, there is a smorgasbord of evidence for this nonhuman intelligence busy playing with humanity.

On one hand, the intelligence seems to attempt to hide but not terribly well. On the other side is an incredible wealth of relevant evidence scattered across different fields of inquiry, though it is so obtuse in nature as to make it hard to process. Considering my certainty that we are in the presence of a nonhuman superintelligence, this incongruity points to a deliberate business of partial revelation incrementally increasing over time. If this force wanted to operate in a truly invisible way, I believe it would do so quite easily.

The film *Minority Report* includes a poignant scene in which two police officers find a room full of evidence implicating their suspect. The investigating agent immediately becomes suspicious:

> Danny Witwer: I worked homicide before I went federal. This is what we call an orgy of evidence. You know how many orgies I had as a homicide cop?
>
> Officer Fletcher: How many?
>
> Danny Witwer: None. This was all arranged.[1]

That is precisely how I am left feeling when considering the wealth of evidence relating to the alien contact scenario currently underway. There are now perhaps millions of people who have experienced alien abduction, psychical contacts, and encounters with anomalous aerial or terrestrial phenomena. It is an orgy of evidence that we have spread before us, and in my opinion, it has been deliberately and meticulously arranged.

While I may be among the few researchers to provide strong evidence of extraterrestrials visiting Earth and modifying humans, I am certainly not the first to suspect we are already in some type of contact event. Unfortunately, the mechanisms are so strange, convoluted, and utterly alien that humanity has mostly failed to recognize what is happening.

If I were to ask the Cheshire Cat from *Alice's Adventures in Wonderland* about his thoughts on these aliens, I suspect the sage advice might be "Nothing would be what it is, because everything would be what it isn't. And contrary wise, what is, it wouldn't be. And what it wouldn't be, it would."[2]

Though it is an important step forward to have scientists collaborate in investigating the alien conundrum, proving extraterrestrials have visited our planet is just one step forward on a more significant journey. The real mystery relates to the nature of reality itself and the interaction between background existence and human consciousness. From the data already offered, it is evident that psychic forces are strongly implicated throughout the interactions with these phenomena.

I am realistic enough to expect a terribly hard job getting materialist reductionist scientists to change their perspectives and engage with this material. I can't help but see them as being akin to Alice talking to the believers represented by the Queen of Hearts:

> Alice: "There's no use trying, one can't believe impossible things."
>
> Queen: "I daresay you haven't had much practice. When I was younger, I always did it for half an hour a day. Why, sometimes I've believed as many as six impossible things before breakfast."[3]

Those of us well used to seemingly impossible things in our own experiences will not struggle so much with engagement in this process. Those who have never encountered the intensely mysterious side of life will likely be unable to adequately process any of this material. It is going to be tough to get the right people looking at the data in a suitably open-minded fashion.

Harvard physicist and great philosopher of science Thomas Kuhn intimately understood the problem currently at hand. It is vital that we understand his findings. Kuhn observed that people and systems are highly resistant to change. Typically change occurs through some degree of force or when it offers a substantial advantage. Any person or system biased toward an existing paradigm will regard any new model as inferior, no matter how much better the new one might be. The bias adherents of opposing paradigms have included favoring the rules of their model to judge the other, resulting in opponents talking over or past each other. According to Kuhn, "Though each may hope to convert the other to his way of seeing his science and its problems, neither may hope to prove his case. The competition between paradigms is not the sort of battle that can be solved by proofs."[4]

No matter how much I may like the idea of leading academics suddenly abandoning positions held for decades, I know it is incredibly unlikely. History tells us that this is not how paradigm change comes. Instead, the young and the open-minded will embrace what seems to be evident to them, irrespective of what any self-appointed authority might say about it, just as we have seen with the rapidly rising belief in alien visitations to Earth. Most believers couldn't care less what some stuffy old Harvard professor has to say about aliens—not unless they happen to agree with them. I predict that within a couple of decades this societal paradigm shift will be complete, with or without engagement from the academic community.

The material offered in this book is intended for all those with eyes to see, ears to hear, and minds open enough to consider new information. If some of these persons happen to be physicists, astronomers, or astrobiologists, so much the better.

In my opinion, this timely manifestation of the intelligence that calls itself Alcheringa is intimately connected to the poor state of our planet and an imminent choice we must all make. Whether it is extraterrestrial, interdimensional, post-biological, or a higher spiritual entity is not the critical matter. What is important is that we as a species listen to the messages and take heed and that we take the proffered hand before it is too late.

HELP CHANGE THE PARADIGM

I hope that this book has been an enjoyable and mind-expanding journey for you and will leave you with food for thought. If you feel that this is a book that other people should read, please take just a couple of moments to leave a short review on Amazon. Every review really helps the book reach somebody else who might gain from reading it.

With your help, this book will help to change the way humanity thinks about the extraterrestrial subject and the human origins story. Let's move disclosure one step closer.

ACKNOWLEDGMENTS

We would like to offer our greatest appreciation to Valerie Barrow for sharing her information and time with us in person, via emails, and through her amazing book, *ALCHERINGA . . . When the First Ancestors Were Created*. Valerie's book acted as a road map for much of this investigation. Special thanks go to William Brown, the head physicist at the Resonance Science Foundation, for his kindly offered thoughts on advanced space travel technologies. I would also like to extend my gratitude to Leonard Farra for sending us his books to explore, which validated some of our own experiences. Our deepest appreciation for his monumental support, goes to Giorgio Tsoukalos. We are both humbled and appreciative of the powerful endorsement offered by the living legend that is Erich von Däniken!

We would also like to express our thanks to John White and Michael Pye, as well as everyone at New Page Books and Red Wheel Weiser.

BIBLIOGRAPHY AND FURTHER READING

Barrow, Valerie. *ALCHERINGA . . . When the First Ancestors Were Created,* Sai Towers Publishing (Bangalore, India), 2002.

Clarke, Arthur C. *2001: A Space Odyssey,* New American Library (New York, US), 1968.

Farra, Leonard. *Genesis Seven,* Vantage Press (New York, US), 1987.

Lovelace, Terry. *Incident at Devils Den, a True Story by Terry Lovelace, Esq.: Compelling Proof of Alien Existence, Alleged USAF Involvement and an Alien Implant Discovered Accidentally on X-Ray,* self-published (US), 2018.

Marciniak, Barbara. *Bringers of the Dawn: Teachings from the Pleiadians,* Bear & Company (Rochester, VT, US), 1992.

Montagu, Ashley. *Coming into Being among the Australian Aborigines: The Procreative Beliefs of the Australian Aborigines,* Routledge & Kegan Paul Books (London, UK), 1974.

Noble, Brian J. *The Third Explanation: The Scientific Case for the Alien Origins of the Human Race,* self-published (London, UK), 2018.

Norbu, Chögyal Namkhai and John Shane. *The Crystal and the Way of Light: Sutra, Tantra and Dzogchen,* Snow Lion Publications (Ithaca, NY, US), 2000.

Swann, Ingo. *Penetration: The Question of Extraterrestrial and Human Telepathy,* Swann-Ryder Productions, Swann-Ryder Productions (UK), 2018.

Von Däniken, Erich. *Chariots of the Gods,* Econ-Verlag (Berlin, Germany), 1968.

REFERENCES

FOREWORD

1   Bruno Vollmert, *Schöpfung* (Freiburg, 1988).

2   Fred Hoyle and Chandra Wickramasinghe, *Die Lebenswolke* (Frankfurt, 1979); Fred Hoyle and Chandra Wickramasinghe, *Evolution aus dem All* (Frankfurt, 1982); and Francis Crick, *Life Itself: Its Origin and Nature* (London, 1982).

3   Albert Schott, *Das Gilgamesch-Epos* (Stuttgart, 1977).

INTRODUCTION

1   Richard Buggs, July 14, 2018, *http://richardbuggs.com.*

CHAPTER 1

1   Tricia Talbert, ed., "Technosignature Search Announced by NASA," NASA, September 25, 2018, https://www.nasa.gov.

2   Martijn Lampert, "Majority of Humanity Say We Are Not Alone in the Universe," Glocalities, accessed January 8, 2020, *www.glocalities.com.*

3   Kathy Frankovic, "Americans Think Ghosts Are More Likely than Aliens on Earth," Economist/YouGov, October 31, 2018, *https://today.yougov.com.*

4   "Do You Believe Earth Has Been Visited by Intelligent Extraterrestrial Alien Life?" Slashdot, accessed January 8, 2020, *https://slashdot.org.*

5   "About 5% of the Reported Unidentified Anomalous Phenomena. . . ." Marie Curie Alumni Association, accessed January 8, 2020, *www.mariecuriealumni.eu*.

6   Catherine Solyom, "UFOs Might Have Been Extra-Terrestrial Vehicles: Retired McGill Professor," *Montreal Gazette*, updated November 14, 2018, *https://montrealgazette.com*.

CHAPTER 2

1   Eli Watkins and Brian Todd, "Former Pentagon UFO Official: 'We May Not Be Alone,'" CNN, updated December 19, 2017, *https://edition.cnn.com*.

2   Jasper Hamill, "Pentagon and MoD Officials Feared UFOs Were Either 'Demonic' or Sent by God, Former Investigators Reveal," May 8, 2018, *https://metro.co.uk*.

3   "The Beginning of To the Stars Academy of Arts & Science," To The Stars Academy of Arts & Science, March 12, 2019, *www.youtube.com*.

4   Luis Elizondo, "'UFOs ARE Real' - Scientific Conference on Anomalous Aerospace Phenomena March 15, 2019," March 19, 2019, *www.youtube.com*.

5   Andy Bloxham, "Aliens Have Deactivated British and US Nuclear Missiles, Say US Military Pilots," *The Telegraph*, September 27, 2010, *www.telegraph.co.uk*.

6   Frank Stalter, "We Have Physical Evidence of UFOs," 2014, *http://ufopartisan.blogspot.com*.

7   Martin A Uman, "Periodically I Hear Stories about Ball Lightning. Does This Phenomenon Really Exist? Could a Ball of Plasma Remain Stable for Several Seconds, as Some Researchers Have Claimed?" *Scientific American*, July 18, 1997, *www.scientificamerican.com*.

8   Uman, "Periodically I Hear Stories."

9   Martin Shough, "The Singular Adventure of Mr Kenneth Arnold," National Aviation Reporting Centre on Anomalous Phenomena (NARCAP), 2010, *www.nicap.org*.

10   Solyom, "UFOs Might."

11 Kevin Knuth, "Are We Alone? The Question Is Worthy of Serious Scientific Study," The Conversation, June 28, 2018, *https://theconversation.com.*

12 Silvano Colombano, "New Assumptions to Guide SETI Research," NASA Ames Research Center, 2018, *https://ntrs.nasa.gov.*

13 Colombano, "New Assumptions."

14 Colombano, "New Assumptions."

15 "Meet Paul Davies, the Man Who'll Greet the Aliens," World Science Festival Staff, April 2014, *www.worldsciencefestival.com.*

CHAPTER 3

1 Ralph Blumenthal, "Alien Nation: Have Humans Been Abducted by Extraterrestrials?" *Vanity Fair*, May 10, 2013, *www.vanityfair.com.*

2 Graham C. L. Davey, "Five Traits That Could Get You 'Abducted by Aliens,'" *Psychology Today*, July 23, 2012, *www.psychologytoday.com.*

3 Davey, "Five Traits."

4 David M. Jacobs, "A Personal Note," International Center for Abduction Research website, *www.ufoabduction.com.*

5 Terry Lovelace, *Incident at Devils Den: A True Story by Terry Lovelace, Esq.: Compelling Proof of Alien Existence, Alleged USAF Involvement and an Alien Implant Discovered Accidentally on X-Ray* (self-pub., 2018).

6 Glenn Gottfried, "Attitudes to Spirituality among Engineering, Technical and Medical Professionals," Ipsos MORI, September 10, 2017, *www.ipsos.com.*

CHAPTER 4

1 Brent Swancer, "Psychic Warriors and Project Jedi," Mysterious Universe, January 28, 2019, *https://mysteriousuniverse.org.*

2 Glenn Garvin, "CIA Files Reveal How U.S. Used Psychics to Spy on Iran," *Miami Herald*, February 10, 2017, *www.miamiherald.com.*

3   Kay Lim, "Psychic Spies: Inside the Government's Secret ESP Program," CBS, August 19, 2018, *www.cbsnews.com.*

4   Ingo Swann, *Penetration: The Question of Extraterrestrial and Human Telepathy* (Ingo Swann Books, 1998).

5   Paul Lester, "Former Apollo Astronaut Calls on the US Government to 'Open Up' about Aliens," *Guardian,* April 22, 2009, *www.theguardian.co.uk.*

6   Lim, "Psychic Spies."

7   Annie Jacobsen, "The U.S. Military Believes People Have a Sixth Sense," *Time,* April 3, 2017, *http://time.com.*

8   Jacobsen, "U.S. Military Believes."

9   Jacobsen, "U.S. Military Believes."

10 Nikita Simonov, "Russian Military Deployed 'Combat Telepathy' in Chechnya, Report Claims," *Moscow Times,* April 3, 2019, *www.themoscowtimes.com.*

CHAPTER 5

1   Mike Wall, "Scientists Find 13 Mysterious Deep-Space Flashes, Including 2nd Known 'Repeater.'" Space.com, January 9, 2019, *www.space.com.*

CHAPTER 6

1   George Dvorsky, "Steven J. Dick: Biological Intelligence Is the Exception, Not the Rule," Sentient Developments, October 2, 2007, *www.sentientdevelopments.com.*

2   *2001: A Space Odyssey,* written by Stanley Kubrick and Arthur C. Clarke, 1968.

3   Paul Gilster, "The Problem with Probes," Centauri Dreams, March 27, 2019, *www.centauri-dreams.org.*

4   "Material of Interest: Magnesium-Zinc-Bismuth," To the Stars Academy website, September 27, 2018, *https://dpo.tothestarsacademy.com.*

5   Judith Simmer-Brown, *Dakini's Warm Breath* (Boulder, CO: Shambhala Publications, 2001), 51–52.

6   Baldwin Spencer and F. J. Gillen, "Chapter IV The Totems," excerpt from *The Native Tribes of North Central Australia* (1899), Sacred Texts website, *www.sacred-texts.com.*

7   M. J. Banias, "Bio-Markers, Brain Structures and Embracing the Strange," Mysterious Universe website, January 12, 2019, *https://mysteriousuniverse.org.*

8   Larry Hardesty, "Computer System Transcribes Words Users 'Speak Silently,'" MIT News website, April 4, 2018, *http://news.mit.edu.*

CHAPTER 7

1   Dr. Alexander Berzin, "Directing Rebirth: The Tibetan Tulku System," transcription of a seminar, Jaegendorf, Germany, June 1996, Study Buddhism by Berzin Archives website, *https://studybuddhism.com.*

2   Susan Schneider, "Alien Minds," chapter 12 in *The Impact of Discovering Life beyond Earth*, ed. Steven J. Dick (Cambridge University Press, 2015), Data Association website, *www.datascienceassn.org.*

3   Floria Thames, "New Year's Eve With(out) Arthur Guirdham," Ellis Taylor website, September 1, 2016, *https://ellisctaylor.com.*

4   Shinsuke Shimojo, Daw-An Wu, and Joseph Kirschvink, "New Evidence for a Human Magnetic Sense that Lets Your Brain Detect the Earth's Magnetic Field," The Conversation, March 18, 2019, *https://theconversation.com.*

5   Paul Kieniewicz, "How Private Are Our Thoughts?" The Scientific & Medical Network, October 1, 2015, *https://explore.scimednet.org.*

6   Kieniewicz, "How Private."

7   Robert F. Service, "DNA Could Store All of the World's Data in One Room," *Science*, March 2, 2017, *www.sciencemag.org.*

8   Katherine Gillespie, "Can We Access the Memories of Our Ancestors through Our DNA?" Vice, December 20, 2016, *www.vice.com.*

9   Arthur C. Clarke, "Hazards of Prophecy: The Failure of Imagination," in *Profiles of the Future: An Inquiry into the Limits of the Possible* (New York: Harper & Row, 1962).

10 "The Alien Observatory—'Advanced Life May Exist in a Form That's Beyond Matter,'" Daily Galaxy, September 30, 2017, *www.soulask.com*.

CHAPTER 8

1   Martijn Lampert, "Majority of Humanity Say We Are Not Alone in the Universe," Glocalities, accessed January 8, 2020, *www.glocalities.com*.

2   "In the Planetary Science Journal *Icarus,* the 'Wow!' Signal of Intelligent Design," Evolution News & Science Today, March 12, 2013, *https://evolutionnews.org*.

3   Maxim Makukov and Vladimir Shcherbak, "SETI in Vivo: Testing the We-Are-Them Hypothesis," *International Journal of Astrobiology,* July 2017, *www.researchgate.net*.

4   Cynthia McKanzie, "Mystery of Our Coded DNA—Who Was the 'Programmer'?" MessageToEagle.com, May 10, 2017, *www.messagetoeagle.com*.

5   "Directed Panspermia Hypothesis," Panspermia-Theory.com, accessed January 10, 2020, *www.panspermia-theory.com*.

6   Tia Ghose, "World's Oldest Fossils Possibly Uncovered in Canada," Live Science, March 1, 2017, *www.livescience.com*.

7   Elizabeth Finkel, "Analysis Suggests Life Sprang on Earth before the Asteroids Stopped Pummelling the Planet," Cosmos website, August 28, 2018, *https://cosmosmagazine.com*.

8   F. H. C. Crick and L. E. Orgel, "Directed Panspermia," *Icarus* 19, no. 3 (July 1973): 341–346, *www.sciencedirect.com*.

9   Lee Speigel, "UK Scientists: Aliens May Have Sent Space Seeds to Create Life on Earth," *Huffington Post,* July 12, 2017, *www.huffingtonpost.com.au*.

10 Helena I. Gomes and Helen Abigail Baxter, "Vanadium: the 'Beautiful Metal' that Stores Energy," May 12, 2016, *https://theconversation.com*.

11 Nalin Chandra Wickramasinghe and Edward J. Steele, "Dangers of Adhering to an Obsolete Paradigm: Could Zika Virus Lead to a Reversal of Human Evolution?" ResearchGate, January 2015, *www.researchgate.net.*

12 Harrison Tasoff, "Interstellar Influenza? Space Viruses Could Reveal Alien Life," Live Science, January 24, 2018, *www.livescience.com.*

13 Edward J. Steele et al., "Cause of Cambrian Explosion—Terrestrial or Cosmic?" *Progress in Biophysics and Molecular Biology* 136 (August 2018): 3–23, *www.sciencedirect.com.*

14 Michael Harner, "Michael Harner's Ayahuasca Experience," excerpt from *The Way of the Shaman*, Acausal Realms website, *https://acausalrealms.wordpress.com.*

15 Michael Harner, *The Way of the Shaman* (San Francisco: Harper & Row, 1980), 4–5.

16 Book of Revelation 12:7–17 (King James Bible).

CHAPTER 9

1 Dom Galeon, "China Claims They Have Actually Created an EM Drive," Futurism, September 20, 2017, *https://futurism.com.*

2 Peter Christoforou, "How Long Would a Spacecraft Take to Reach Proxima Centauri?" Astronomy Trek website, September 24, 2016, *www.astronomytrek.com.*

3 Valerie Barrow, *ALCHERINGA . . . When the First Ancestors Were Created* (self-pub., CreateSpace, 2002).

4 Barrow, *ALCHERINGA.*

5 William Brown, Resonance Foundation, personal correspondence.

6 Nola Taylor Redd, "What Is Wormhole Theory?" SPACE.com, October 21, 2017, *www.space.com.*

7 Matt Visser et al., "Traversable Wormholes with Arbitrarily Small Energy Condition Violations," *Physical Review Letters* 90, 201102 (2003), *https://arxiv.org.*

8   Gaurav Khanna, "Maybe You Really Can Use Black Holes to Travel the Universe," Astronomy.com, January 29, 2019, *www.astronomy.com.*

9   "Cree Mythology Written in the Stars," CBC Radio, January 15, 2016, *www.cbc.ca.*

10 L. Farra, *Genesis Seven* (New York: Vantage Press, 1987), 5–9.

11 "Seven Sisters," Kitezh website, accessed January 10, 2020, *www.kitezh.com.*

CHAPTER 10

1   R. H. Charles, trans., *The Book of Enoch*, chapter 14:10–12 (1917), Sacred-Texts.com, *www.sacred-texts.com.*

2   Rupert Hawkesley, "Britain's Roswell: What Really Happened in the Rendlesham Forest UFO Incident?" *Telegraph*, December 31, 2018, *www.telegraph.co.uk.*

3   Valerie Barrow, *ALCHERINGA . . . When the First Ancestors Were Created* (self-pub., CreateSpace, 2002).

4   Valerie Barrow, "The Moldavite Story," Valerie Barrow website, November 12, 2011, *www.valeriebarrow.com.*

5   Frantisek "Tektites Dating—Determining the Age of Moldavites," AboutMoldavites.com, February 12, 2014, *www.aboutmoldavites.com.*

6   Valerie Barrow, "Moldavite Is the Remains of the Mothership Rexegena," The Mystery Schools website, *http://valeriebarrow.com.*

7   Robin Andrews, "Massive Missing Meteorite Impact Crater Hunt Narrows After Glassy Debris Uncovered in Antarctica," IFLScience!, April 10, 2018, *www.iflscience.com.*

8   Christopher Fry, "3D Laser Imaging and Modeling of Iron Meteorites and Tektites," Figure 1 (master's thesis, Carleton University, 2013), ResearchGate website, *www.researchgate.net.*

9   "Tektites (Australites)," Earth Science Australia website, *http://earthsci.org.*

10 E. W. Adams and R. M. Huffaker, "Aerodynamic Analysis of Tektites and Their Parent Bodies," January 1, 1962, NASA Technical Reports Server website, *https://ntrs.nasa.gov.*

11 Adams and Huffaker, "Aerodynamic Analysis."

12 "World Tektite."

13 William A. Cassidy, "Australite Investigations and Their Bearing on the Tektite Problem," *Meteoritics* 1, no. 4 (June 1956): 426, *https://doi.org/10.1111/j.1945-5100.1956.tb01378.x.*

14 S. R. Taylor, "The Chemical Composition of Australites," Geochimica et Cosmochimica Acta 26, no. 7 (July 1962): 685–722, *www.researchgate.net.*

15 Dean R. Chapman and Howard K. Larsen, *The Lunar Origin of Tektites*, Technical Note D-1556 (Moffett Field, Calif.: Ames Research Center, February 1963), *https://ntrs.nasa.gov.*

16 J. A. O'Keefe, *The Origin of Tektites*, Technical Note D-490 (Goddard Space Flight Center, November 1960), *https://ntrs.nasa.gov.*

17 Peter S. Fiske et al., "Layered Tektites of Southeast Asia: Field Studies in Central Laos and Vietnam," *Meteoritics & Planetary Science* 34 (1999): 757–761, *https://doi.org/10.1111/j.1945-5100.1999.tb01388.x.*

18 Norm Lehrman, "The Futrell 458.3 gm Hainan Muong Nong: Seventh Sojourn," *Meteorite Times Magazine,* January 1, 2017, *www.meteorite-times.com.*

19 "The Black Stone of Mecca: History and Symbolism," Psy-Minds.com, accessed January 10, 2020, *https://psy-minds.com.*

CHAPTER 11

1 Valerie Barrow, *ALCHERINGA . . . When the First Ancestors Were Created* (self-pub., CreateSpace, 2002).

2 Sean Martin, "Multiple Meteors Hit Earth Causing Devastation Including Tsunamis and Huge Earthquakes," *Express,* February 23, 2016, *www.express.co.uk.*

3   Flavio Barbiero, "On the Possibility of Instantaneous Shifts of the Poles," Graham Hancock website, May 17, 2006, *https:// grahamhancock.com*.

4   Harald Franzen, "Why Venus Spins the Wrong Way," *Scientific American*, June 15, 2001, *www.scientificamerican.com*.

5   Jason Major, "Venus Spinning Slower than Thought—Scientists Stumped," *National Geographic*, February 15, 2012, *https://news.nationalgeographic.com*.

6   Thomas B. Chalk et al., "Causes of Ice Age Intensification across the Mid-Pleistocene Transition," *Proceedings of the National Academy of Sciences of the United States of America* website, December 12, 2017, *www.pnas.org*.

7   Simon Worrall, "Earth's Poles Will Eventually Flip, So What Then?" *National Geographic*, February 1, 2018, *https://news .nationalgeographic.com*.

8   Stephanie Pappas, "An Electro-Blob under Africa May Be 'Ground Zero' for Earth's Magnetic Field Reversal," Live Science, March 7, 2018, *www.livescience.com*.

CHAPTER 12

1   Spanish Foundation for Science and Technology, "A Cosmic Gorilla Effect Could Blind the Detection of Aliens," Phys.org, April 11, 2018, *https://phys.org*.

2   "Meet Paul Davies, the Man Who'll Greet the Aliens," World Science Festival Staff, April 2014, *www.worldsciencefestival .com*.

3   Samuel Arbesman, "If You Were a Secret Message, Where in the Human Genome Would You Hide?" Nautilus website, April 1, 2015, *http://nautil.us*.

4   Katherine S. Pollard, "What Makes Us Different?" *Scientific American*, November 1, 2012, *www.scientificamerican.com*.

5   Katherine S. Pollard, "Decoding Human Accelerated Regions," The Scientist website, August 1, 2016, *www.the-scientist.com*.

6   Valerie Barrow, *ALCHERINGA . . . When the First Ancestors Were Created* (self-pub., CreateSpace, 2002).

7   Barrow, *ALCHERINGA.*

8   Jane J. Lee, "World's Oldest Genome Sequenced From 700,000-Year-Old Horse DNA," *National Geographic,* November 7, 2017, *www.nationalgeographic.co.uk.*

9   "Genetic Difference: Genotype and Phenotype," Australian Law Reform Commission website, July 23, 2010, *www.alrc.gov.au.*

10 Mark Moore, "How the Hobbits Kept Their Tools as They Shrank into Island Life," The Conversation website, June 8, 2016, *https://theconversation.com.*

11 Jef Akst, "Ancient Humans More Diverse?" The Scientist website, January 18, 2010, *www.the-scientist.com.*

12 Chad D. Huff, "New Look at Archaic DNA Rewrites Human Evolution Story," The University of Utah website, August 2017, *https://unews.utah.edu.*

13 James P. Noonan et al., "Sequencing and Analysis of Neanderthal Genomic DNA," *Science* 314, 5802 (2006), *www.osti.gov.*

14 R. M. Harding, et al., "Archaic African and Asian Lineages in the Genetic Ancestry of Modern Humans," *American Journal of Human Genetics* 60, no. 4 (April 1997): 772–789, *www.ncbi.nlm.nih.gov.*

CHAPTER 13

1   J. W. IJdo et al., "Origin of Human Chromosome 2: an Ancestral Telomere-Telomere Fusion," *Proceedings of the National Academy of Sciences of the United States of America* 88, no. 20 (October 15, 1991): 9051–9055, *www.ncbi.nlm.nih.gov.*

2   Dennis Venema, "Denisovans, Humans and the Chromosome 2 Fusion," BiosLogos website, September 6, 2012, *https://biologos.org.*

3   Adam Benton, "Adam's Chromosomes Were Fused (and He Lived Earlier than We Thought)," Filthy Monkey Men website, November 8, 2016, *www.filthymonkeymen.com.*

4   Jerry Bergman and Jeffrey Tomkins, "The Chromosome 2 Fusion Model of Human Evolution—Part 1: Re-Evaluating the Evidence," Creation.com, 2012, *https://creation.com.*

5   Michio Kaku, "Mankind Has Stopped Evolving," Big Think website, February 15, 2011, *http://bigthink.com*.

6   Manuel Ruiz Rejón, "The Origin of the Human Species: A Chromosome Fusion?" Open Mind website, January 17, 2017, *www.bbvaopenmind.com*.

7   Ruiz Rejón, "The Origin."

8   Pawel Stankiewicz, "One Pedigree We All May Have Come From—Did Adam and Eve Have the Chromosome 2 Fusion?" *Molecular Cytogenetics* 9, no. 72 (2016), *www.ncbi.nlm .nih.gov*.

9   Helen Briggs, "DNA Clue to How Humans Evolved Big Brains," BBC News, December 7, 2016, *www.bbc.com*.

10 "Bigger Brains: Complex Brains for a Complex World," Smithsonian website, updated January 16, 2019, *http:// humanorigins.si.edu*.

11 Tia Ghose, "'Big Brain' Gene Allowed for Evolutionary Expansion of Human Neocortex," *Scientific American*, February 27, 2015, *www.scientificamerican.com*.

12 "What Made Us Human: 'Unique' Evolution Gene Found," *The Sydney Morning Herald*, November 15, 2012, *www.smh .com.au*.

13 Anne Trafton, "Neuroscientists Identify Key Role of Language Gene," MIT News website, September 15, 2014, *http:// news.mit.edu*.

14 M. J. Banias, "Bio-Markers, Brain Structures and Embracing the Strange," Mysterious Universe website, January 12, 2019, *https://mysteriousuniverse.org*.

15 Ronald Bailey, "Making Malaria Mosquitoes Extinct Using Engineered Gene-Drives," Reason website, February 20, 2019, *https://reason.com*.

CHAPTER 14

1   Pat Lee Shipman, "Why Is Human Childbirth So Painful?" *American Scientist* 101, no. 6 (November–December 2013): 426, *www.americanscientist.org*.

2   "Earliest Known Fossil of the Genus *Homo* Dates to 2.8 to 2.75 Million Years Ago," Penn State, HeritageDaily website, March 5, 2015, *www.heritagedaily.com*.

3   Megan Y. Dennis et al., "Human-Specific Evolution of Novel SRGAP2 Genes by Incomplete Segmental Duplication," *Cell* 149, no. 4 (May 2012): 912–22, *www.ncbi.nlm.nih.gov*.

4   Jeremy Griffith, "Chapter 5:9 Sexual Selection for Integrativeness Explains Neoteny," from *Freedom: The End of The Human Condition* (WTM Publishing and Communications, 2016), World Transformation Movement website, *www.humancondition.com*.

5   Lyudmila Trut et al., "Animal Evolution during Domestication: The Domesticated Fox as a Model," *Bioessays* 31, no. 3 (March 2009): 349–60, *www.ncbi.nlm.nih.gov*.

6   "Did Humans Domesticate Themselves?" Universidad de Barcelona website, February 15, 2018, *www.ub.edu*.

7   Nathan Lents, *Human Errors: A Panorama of Our Glitches, from Pointless Bones to Broken Genes* (Boston: Houghton Mifflin Harcourt, 2018).

CHAPTER 15

1   World Science Festival, "Who Is Out There: Why Alien 'Life' May Be Weirder than We Imagine," June 7, 2018, https://www.youtube.com.

2   Percentages in this section are from Damian Carrington, "Insect Collapse: 'We Are Destroying Our Life Support Systems,'" *Guardian*, January 15, 2019, *www.theguardian.com*; statements about causes come from Marlowe Hood, "World Seeing 'Catastrophic Collapse' of Insects: Study," Phys.org, February 11, 2019, *https://phys.org*.

3   Brian J. Noble, *How Will Our Children Survive* (self-pub., 2019).

4   Tess Riley, "Just 100 Companies Responsible for 71% of Global Emissions, Study Says," *Guardian*, July 10, 2017, *www.theguardian.com*.

5   Timothy Revell, "AI Will Be Able to Beat Us at Everything by 2060, Say Experts," New Scientist website, May 31, 2017, *www.newscientist.com.*

AFTERWORD

1   *Minority Report,* short story written by Philip K. Dick, screenplay written by Scott Frank and Jon Cohen (2002).
2   Lewis Carroll, *Alice's Adventures in Wonderland* (London: MacMillan, 1865).
3   Carroll, *Alice's Adventures in Wonderland.*
4   "Paradigm Change," Thwink.org, accessed January 10, 2020, *www.thwink.org.*

ABOUT THE AUTHORS

Bruce Fenton is an information systems professional who has dedicated more than twenty years to the research of scientific anomalies and ancient mysteries. His books have regularly appeared in the Amazon bestseller positions in their relevant categories. Best known for leading a Science Channel expedition into the Caucasus Mountains, Bruce played a key role in the investigation of a mysterious ancient megalithic structure in Ecuador's Amazon jungle. Bruce has been featured on dozens of radio shows and is a regular contributor to several large online media platforms. His writings on early human migrations attracted the endorsement of luminaries such as bestselling author Graham Hancock, who had this to say of his work, "Indeed, it has the potential—although I cannot promise that this potential will be fulfilled—to rewrite history."

Daniella Fenton is a professional horse broker respected in her industry for her incredible knowledge of equine anatomy, genetics, and bloodlines. Daniella is a gifted spiritual medium, regression therapist, and empathic counselor. She spent five years developing shamanic healing skills in the Ecuadorian Andes alongside a number of local curanderos.

Notably, Daniella holds government certification to practice shamanism in Peru. Daniella has been featured on many radio shows, and her research work has appeared on websites around the globe.